Natural Style
for GARDENS

Natural Style
for GARDENS

FRANCESCA GREENOAK

MITCHELL BEAZLEY

For Barbara, whose garden is an inspiration

NATURAL STYLE FOR GARDENS

First published in Great Britain 1998 by Mitchell Beazley,
an imprint of Reed Consumer Books Limited,
Michelin House, 81 Fulham Road,
London SW3 6RB

ISBN 1-84000-031-7 ✓

A CIP catalogue copy of this book is available
from the British Library

Executive Editor: Alison Starling
Executive Art Editor: Vivienne Brar
Senior Editor: Michèle Byam
Art Editor: Debbie Myatt
Production: Rachel Staveley
Picture Research: Emily Hedges
Illustrator: Vanessa Luff
Index: Ann Barrett

Set in Garamond

Printed and bound in China by
Toppan Printing Company Limited

CONTENTS

WHAT IS A NATURAL GARDEN?

The natural garden acknowledges the individuality of the garden terrain and the character and period of the house, working with nature to create an orderly exuberance of plants and texture. Focus is placed upon associations of wild species of plants that are easy to grow and garden cultivars that will naturalize readily. Gardening in a natural style is a refinement of the skills of using plants that are well suited to the conditions you are working with, so that with a light and lyrical hand you can orchestrate a succession of flowers and foliage that flows with both the weather and the seasons.

LEFT **A drift of gaillardias (***Gaillardia* x *grandiflora***) growing with red-flowered** *Salvia microphylla* **make a dazzling high summer eruption of colour. Both have long, late-flowering seasons and tolerate poor soil.**

WORKING WITH NATURE

No garden is dull: even the smallest ones have several different habitats and microclimates within them. There will be a shady place, a dry, sunny hot spot, maybe a pool or at least an area of dampness. There could be a hedge or a wall, possibly some paving. Almost all of these – in fact everything except rich, fertile loamy beds – are usually regarded as problem places, but in fact each has a specific flora that will thrive there, opening a wealth of possibility.

This book explores a garden's underlying potential and how to use that potential to design a garden that suits your own personal taste. There are over 60,000 plants currently in cultivation in the temperate world: more than enough to suit every soil and situation. If you match the plant to the place and choose those that are native or that readily naturalize, you are more likely to end up with a healthy, thriving garden than if you try to grow shade-loving plants in the sun or make changes to soils in order to grow plants that are unsuitable for your local soil and climate.

A natural garden of this kind contains plants that are either hardy natives or introductions that have taken readily to gardens in temperate parts of the world, naturalizing and self-seeding, or spreading without the need for special attention. It takes its cue from the natural environment, but uses plant species that come from similar habitats in different places throughout the temperate world. A natural style involves selecting from the plant composition of the natural landscape and scaling it so that it achieves an effect that pleases the eye and minimizes labour.

LANDSCAPE

It is more rewarding, as well as easier, to work with the forces of nature. Take a look at your garden within the wider landscape. Some gardens already have a dominating character, such as a dry coastal strip, peaty marshy ground or a high-altitude rocky region. Gardens such as these are easy to identify because you can see wild plants that are blooming in the area, and so proceed to grow a further range of species with similar requirements. Seaside gardens, for example, require planting that will survive salt winds, yet the maritime climate is generally milder, allowing you to consider plants that could be at risk inland. Even in such apparently single-minded gardens, however, there will be variation and possibilities for extending the range of plants with others from places elsewhere with similar conditions.

As most people live in either urban areas or places that have been built on for many years, it is often difficult to know what kind of soils and conditions you are dealing with. It is here that existing vegetation and even weeds can help, each signalling the state and quality of the soil in which they are growing. The absence of a natural landscape does not mean you are at a disadvantage – urban landscapes have their own special character and temperatures are generally higher, which means that less hardy plants will thrive.

BELOW Stone steps set into a hillside, colonized with woodland mosses, ferns, sedges and woodland-edge flowering plants such as green alkanet (*Pentaglottis sempervirens*), foxglove (*Digitalis purpurea*) and red campion (*Silene dioica*). These type of plants naturalize readily and should be planted, as here, in open groupings.

OPPOSITE Grasses continue to look glamorous throughout the autumn and winter months. Here, pampas (*Cortaderia*) teamed with yucca looks sensational against reddening maples.

NATURAL BALANCE

In the natural garden, climate as well as geography must be taken into account. Plants have their own specialisms. Some, ideally suited to mild, temperate regions, need a long season to flower and fruit, while others thrive in the short but intensive summers of high latitudes. One range of species (the native British flora, for example) can cope with winters that alternate between cold and wet. Other groups, such as alpines, perish under such conditions but will survive a greater degree of cold, provided that they have a blanket of snow, while species with special xerophytic characteristics perform best in great heat.

Gardening in a more natural way you learn to note plants that are comfortable in their site and soil and that will grow healthily without the need for artificial feeding. Far too many gardens at present impose preconceived designs on land for which they are not appropriate. The outcome is usually either failure or, at best, a mediocre result, demanding of both labour and fertilizer and yet ultimately unsatisfying. Plants that are species or close to a species – rather than an artificial hybrid – generally grow without much interference. You should give them extra water while they are getting established, but after that watering should either be unnecessary or minimal. The most important thing is to plant properly by choosing a congenial spot, giving the plant enough space, minimizing competition from grass and weeds while the root system is settling in, and keeping up the general fertility of the soil with compost (home-made or commercially available composted bark). When treated this way, most plants will thrive with the minimum of intervention.

The artificially produced cultivars that are bred for a prodigious show of flowers require high amounts of fertilizer. Amongst such unnaturally

BELOW **Warmth, scent and texture in an informal grouping ranged around a sundial under the high summer sun: French lavender (***Lavandula stoechas***), spiky *Eryngium giganteum*, *Helianthus* and the velvet, dark red, strongly perfumed gallica rose 'Tuscany Superb'.**

floriferous subjects are African marigolds, petunias, impatiens and pot chrysanthemums. Not only does much of the high-octane fertilizer required get washed away into the water system, but it produces a rapid sappy growth that tends to attract aphids. There is a fertilizer-pesticide equation in such a regime and the aphids need to be sprayed with pesticide. On the other hand, if grown in a more natural way, a normally flower-rich species regulates its own growth and flowering and is able to put on a good display of bloom without artificial aid. Plants grown in this way are not only less stressed but attract fewer pests.

GARDEN HEALTH

It is perfectly possible to have a healthy and blooming garden without having to continually drench it with chemicals. There is now a strong body of research to demonstrate the benefit of a more natural approach, although some gardeners, indoctrinated by propaganda that implies that no garden could survive without pesticides, find this hard to believe. In practice, once a good balance of plants of different kinds has been established, you are unlikely to be troubled by pests or diseases to any significant extent. A healthy mixed economy that supports a range of insects is always better than a monoculture that tends to attract specialized pests in large numbers. As doubts are raised about the safety of a number of garden chemicals, many people are either switching to a minimum-dose regime or doing without them altogether; a practical experience that should serve as a model to other gardeners.

An important pointer to the health of any garden is its wildlife. I find the presence of insects in the garden has become one of my greatest pleasures. Although they are not as easy to identify as birds, with a good insect field guide it is possible to get fairly close. It is fascinating to discover that your hedge is home to the exquisite little brimstone moth (*Gonepteryx rhamni*) or that the ivy on the wall provides a source of food and shelter for a number of birds and butterflies. In many parts of the USA it is possible to attract hummingbirds as well as butterflies into a garden, and a wildflower seed company has recently introduced a special mixture designed to attract these beautiful creatures.

It is useful to get the measure of the animals with whom you share your garden (*see pp.116–129*). Some you will want to encourage, while others you may feel inclined to tolerate only in small numbers – I feel this way about the beautiful magpie moths (*Abraxas*

grossulariata) that feed on currant and gooseberry bushes, although a few of the yellow, black and white looper caterpillars do little harm. I am happy to tolerate a few holed leaves for the sake of the pretty pied and orange adult moths, all of whom have slightly different patterning. On the other hand, the handsome, scarlet lily beetle (*Lilioceris lilii*) is on the increase and, unlike the magpie moth, extremely destructive. It is important to control these pests, since the unpleasant messy larvae will make short work of lily leaves. There is a similar problem with the species of sawfly that attack a range of plants. The one pest I especially watch out for in spring is the Solomon's seal sawfly (*Phymatocera atterrima*). If left to its own devices, this little insect can reduce plant leaves to skeletons.

Aphids can be a problem, but if you have a good population of ladybirds and hoverflies it is really not worth trying to get rid of these pests, except in the case of any plants that are especially at risk. I once experimented by treating one half of a large, aphid-infested rambling rose with a soft-soap spray (which effectively disposed of the aphids), while leaving the other half untreated. A few weeks later, when the insect predators had been at work, there was absolutely no difference in foliage or flowering between the treated and untreated halves of the rose. In the USA and southern parts of Europe praying mantises are also voracious eaters of aphids and many other plant pests.

ABOVE **Magpie moths** (*Abraxas grossulariata*) **vary in their patterning and are such handsome insects that it seems a shame to persecute them. They lay their eggs on currant bushes, but the damage they cause is usually negligible.**

ASSESSING YOUR GARDEN

Even the most conventional garden can take on a more natural style that takes account of its fundamental characteristics. No changes need be hurried; the transition can be gradual or partial, entirely according to the owner's taste. The first thing to do is to take a long look at the garden as a whole, trying to determine its possibilities within its local environment. It is certainly necessary to take account of the immediate surroundings. A rambling cottage garden, perfectly acceptable in the middle of the country, looks rather silly in urban surroundings, while a prairie-type meadow with long grasses may not be acceptable to neighbours who worry about weed seeds or a fire hazard. There may indeed be local safety regulations with regard to mowing grass.

Evaluate the garden in its own terms for the different habitats that are present within it – even if they are not all currently exploited (you may like to use the chart on the opposite page as a guide to some of the differences you should look out for). Next, consider what you might like to add to the garden. If you do not have a pond or stream, should you think of making one? If you do, where would it fit most naturally? Can you assist any of the other microclimates you find in the garden to develop, by introducing plants of a character that is appropriate to them? Perhaps there are wild plant communities in your part of the country that you would like to have growing in your garden? (However, remember that if you want truly local genetic strains, you should take seed sparingly and raise them yourself – never dig out wild plants.)

PLANTS FOR PLACES

The information and suggestions in this book, together with your own observations of wild places, should enable you to develop some ideas about how you want to proceed. If you have an area of dry shade, for example, you will be looking for plants that grow best in that situation, blend well with each other and fit into the rest of the garden. Examine the plants you already have and see which ones are growing well and therefore obviously suit the terrain. The plants you finally decide upon should be of appropriate height and proportions for the garden as a whole. All the ideas you intend to take forward should be based on how you have related the elements within the garden, both to each other and to the character of the outside landscape.

It can be tricky to identify the exact conditions of any piece of ground: the degree of fertility; whether it is acid, neutral or alkaline in character; how well drained it is; and the degree of dryness or moistness. You may find help in an unexpected quarter – weeds can be very useful in indicating growing conditions. Plantains (*Plantago*) and sorrel (*Rumex acetosa* and *R. acetosella*), for example, indicate acidic soil, while pansies (*Viola*) and poppies (*Papaver rhoeas*) are evidence of alkaline conditions. Chickweed (*Stellaria media*) is a sign of neutral and well-drained soil, which is also evidenced by most speedwells (*Veronica*), goosegrass (*Galium aparine*) and henbit dead nettle (*Lamium amplexicaule*), whereas summer-flowering weeds on the increase indicate low fertility. Stinging nettles (*Urtica*), sow thistles (*Sonchus*) and ground elder (*Aegopodium podagraria*) signify high levels of nitrogen, while vetches (*Vicia*) and clovers (*Trifolium*) indicate a deficit. Equally, poor drainage can be demonstrated by an invasion of creeping buttercup (*Ranunculus repens*), horsetails (*Equisetum*) and coltsfoot (*Tussilago farfara*).

BELOW **This garden links to the surrounding farm and woodland landscape by means of an open picket fence. Informal plantings of** *Crambe cordifolia* **and poplar (***Populus***) lead the eye naturally to the countryside beyond.** *Crambe*, **with its open-branched, white inflorescences, is very attractive to bees.**

GARDEN HABITAT CHECKLIST

Check how many of these habitats you have
(or could initiate) and use the relevant section
of this book to help you develop them:

- **Beds** loamy, dry, moist; acid/neutral/alkaline
- **Lawn** grass only; older lawn grasses/some
  wildflowers
- **Dry shade** under wall/hedge/under trees
- **Damp shade** damp wall/north-facing moist area
- **Damp places** lawn or bed; by tap, pool or
  boggy area
- **Sunny places** bed/wall in the sun/bank
- **Trees** heavy shade/light shade
- **Longer grass** sun/shade
- **Walls** height/material/age; existing flora
- **Fences and Trellises** material/height/shelter
- **Banks** natural/man-made; shady/bright; dry/wet
- **Pools, Ponds, Streams** in sun/shade; still/moving

LEFT A woodland
community in a city centre
thrives with the minimum
of attention. The plants
include green alkanet
(*Pentaglottis sempervirens*),
yellow archangel (*Lamium
galeobdolon*), hybrid
bluebell (*Hyacinthoides*)
and spotted dead nettle
(*Lamium maculatum*),
while ivy winds around
the railings and trees.

BELOW Dry, poor soil
supports a colourful
mixture of plants,
including purple *Veronica
spicata*, blue harebells
(*Campanula rotundifolia*),
thyme (*Thymus*), red
valerian (*Centranthus
ruber*), yellow corn
marigold (*Chrysanthemum
segetum*), knapweed
(*Centaurea nigra*) and
toadflax (*Linaria vulgaris*).

ACHIEVING HARMONY IN THE GARDEN

The habitats upon which a natural style is based may be distant from each other in the natural landscape, but in a garden they butt up against each other and need to be linked or given points of transition in terms of planting and design. A good garden must have congruity so that its parts blend together to form a harmonious whole. You also need to consider the style and period of the house to which the garden belongs, as well as the wider landscape outside.

The moment you enter a garden, you should be able to detect a distinct character and how that reflects the interests and personality of the owner. The most significant plants, an unusual style of plant associations, the flow of the design and the particular way the challenges of terrain and place are met reflect the preferences of the individual gardener. It is often the case that genius is expressed in more difficult situations, such as when a poky town yard is made into a magical foliage garden, when difficult soil conditions have prompted innovative and curious combinations of special plants, or in gardens that defy extremes of climate, such as short, hot summers and bitterly cold winters.

Just as a piece of music can sound quite different depending on the performer, so plants will look and behave differently according to who is handling them and where they are planted. There is endless scope for originality and individuality, although it is also useful to visit other gardens, read books, and go to flower shows in order to find out what is available and how other people plant and design. Then clear your mind and plan your garden according to your own vision.

Gardeners have always loved the sensuality of the garden and some, such as the seventeenth-century British writer William Lawson, author of the classic *The New Orchard and Garden*, have revelled in the intellectual pleasures that a garden affords. This is surely the clue to a garden that brings full satisfaction – a lifelong relationship in which your interests develop and your knowledge extends as you experiment with new plants and schemes.

One element that is almost completely absent from most writing about plants and gardens is the suggestion that the gardener as an individual might develop not only in knowledge and experience of gardening, but also in terms of personal, physical and psychological appreciation. With the increase in asthmatic complaints that depress the power to smell, fewer people are able to appreciate scents. Even non-asthmatics often hunch their shoulders, screw their necks forward and gasp when they are about to smell something, thus preventing their sense organs from functioning properly. Fuller appreciation is likely when you simply allow the scent to flood your normal breathing, keeping the mind and the senses completely alive to the beauty of the different strands of scent. It is the same with the other senses. If you allow your hands to become hardened and calloused and the joints stiff with overtension, you lose the acute sensibility of the fingertips. If you strain your eyes to see everything, you are more likely to give yourself a headache than refine your perception of texture and colour. If you can feel relaxed and happy in your garden, you are more likely to extend your appreciation.

BELOW **A hillside garden tumbling to a pool of yellow flag and variegated iris. The foxgloves on the edge of the trees give way to drier ground and *Lychnis coronaria*. The effect looks unplanned, but there is a careful balance of shrubs and flowers, dwarf conifers and other evergreens.**

OPPOSITE **A damp grassy path dominated by informal planting of *Primula florindae* and blue *Meconopsis baileyi*. To the right are the demure crimson-brown blooms of another choice woodlander, *Trillium sessile*. Dotted amongst the shrubs are types of woodland flora, including bluebells and Turk's-cap lilies.**

A GARDEN OF HARMONIOUS SENSUALITY

Scent is one of the most compelling of the senses, working on the subconscious directly and sometimes unnervingly, conjuring up ideas, memories and desires. It is a powerful element in garden composition. Some of the strong spring scents, such as winter honeysuckle (*Lonicera*), narcissus and hyacinth, are made for cool frosty air. If you bring these plants indoors their impact is so strong that it becomes almost disagreeable. On the other hand, the fleeting scent of snowdrops (*Galanthus nivalis*), the tang of daffodils (*Narcissus pseado-narcissus*) and the sweetness of grape hyacinths (*Muscari armeniacum*) are better appreciated in warm indoor conditions.

There are enough scented plants not only to take you through the entire year but to grow without the fuss and bother associated with the horticulturally demanding and more conventionally admired specimens, such as hybrid roses. If you want roses, there are many types that grow readily in semi-natural conditions and are at their happiest left to

themselves. These include wild species with light sweet scents, such as the dog rose (*Rosa canina*) and the field rose (*R. arvensis*), both of which will ramble cheerfully in a hedge. One of my favourite roses is the sweet briar (*R. eglanteria*), because of the rich, musky apple scent of its leaves – although this is a species that, as with other imports from the Old World, ran riot in New Zealand. I believe that some of the delightful cultivars, developed mainly by Lord Penzance in the 1890s, may be better behaved in those regions, but in general sweet briars behave well in temperate conditions. Especially delightful is the one named 'Lord Penzance' after its breeder. It has sweetly scented foliage (although the pink 'Lady Penzance' is stronger in this respect) and small, delicately sweet flowers in an unusual shade of buff-rose, blending into a rich golden centre.

The rugosas are also to be treasured for their glossy apple-green foliage and scented single and double flowers. The species *Rosa rugosa*, originally from northern China, Japan and Korea, has flowers that range from pale to dark pink. *R. r. alba* is also highly scented, with pure white flowers, while the outstanding hybrid 'Blanche Double de Coubert' is equally fragrant, with almost double white flowers set against dark foliage. All of these rugosas possess the very useful twin qualities of thriving in poorer soils and shaded conditions and of repeat flowering.

THE TANGIBLE FRAMEWORK

The shapes and textures within gardens are not simply for admiring at a distance. Even if you can find very little time actually to sit and relax within a garden you can still enjoy them. Plant scented herbs and favourite flowers by the side of the most used paths, so that you can reach out to rub the foliage to release their scents each time you pass by. Thymes, mints and chamomile may be tucked between stone flags or paving, or bedded down by doorsteps, so that the scent is released when anyone walks over them. Some leaves and petals are irresistible – the soft silver rabbit ears of *Stachys byzantina*, the velvet leaves of *Alchemilla* species and the soft petals of the rose are all lovely when cupped in the hand.

Unfortunately, a large number of gardeners get arthritis in later life. This condition is exacerbated by continuous overtension in the muscles of their shoulders, arms and hands. The garden is an ideal place to learn how to release such tension and enjoy

BELOW **Midsummer-blooming lilies of the Asiatic hybrid type characteristically hold their heads upwards. Among the best are 'Apollo' and 'Sterling Star', both white and reliable, with bowl-shaped flowers.**

being re-educated into the sense of touch. Run your hands quietly over the bark of a tree; investigate foliage gently, noting the softness of young lime leaves, the leatheriness of oak; cup your hand to feel the life in the unfurling seedpods of an impatiens or caper spurge *(Euphorbia lathyrus)*.

Bear in mind that it is not just your hands that are sensitive. Explore the lawn in bare feet or give your toes a treat by walking through chamomile or mint. Winter sunshine is soft and warming, even through a shirt or jumper, and it is pleasant to feel a sense of the elements on your face, such as a spring breeze or a soft drizzle. The backs of the hands are also sensitive; if you learn to listen to their message, you can feel the differences in the strength of the wind as it blows through the branches of a tree, the fleeting touch of an insect or the chill of snowflakes.

Some trees with ornamental bark – shiny-barked species of cherry, birch and maple – are the better for being rubbed as this keeps them shiny and bright and free from algae. It is easy to neglect this service and let the glorious bark of these types of trees turn dowdy, so if you have a tree with ornamental or flaking bark, be sure to stroke it as you pass by.

BEAUTY AND TASTE

Plants grown for eating can also be of exceptional beauty. Apple trees, quince and medlars, apricots, plums and cherries all have great decorative value, from their early leaves through to their blossoms and ripe fruits. Allowing for climatic variations, there is almost without exception a fruit tree that will grow well and need very little attention. The same applies to bushes such as gooseberries or, if you have acidic soil, bilberries or blueberries. Gooseberries are a greatly undervalued fruit. They come into bright green leaf very early in the season, when they are superb if underplanted with scented, flame-coloured or yellow tulips; the fruits may be used early, when they are still sour, or left to ripen to sweet fullness in ivory, gold, green or red.

Many salad greens are not out of place in an ornamental garden. In my smallest gardens I have grown the oak-leaved and 'Salad Bowl' lettuces in the flower borders, where they were much admired. Lamb's lettuce and land cress will also fit into odd spaces among flowers. Shallots, the easiest of onions to grow, make neat clusters, while climbing beans are also pleasing to the eye. Indeed runner beans were valued as ornamental plants before they became popular as a green vegetable.

LEFT Tree trunks have a beauty of their own. Some, such as the birch *Betula ermanii*, are stars in their own right, the bark colour ranging from buff-pink to creamy white. The catkins are golden brown, the autumn leaves yellow-gold. Coppiced birches make multiple trunks, such as the one shown here.

BELOW *Clematis* 'Bill Mackenzie' is a vigorous climber. From mid summer to autumn it produces abundant small, yellow flowers, which are followed by large seedheads, at first silken and then fluffy. It is thought to be a hybrid between two 'orange peel' types of clematis.

Strawberry plants, especially the delicate and piquant wild and alpine strawberries, are a distinct asset in an informal garden. Growing delicious fruits, herbs and vegetables is also a means of sharing the joys of the garden with children. It is not difficult to grow a range of edible fruits, flowers and salad greens that will extend throughout the year and fit comfortably with a naturalistic style.

HARMONIES AND SOUNDS

While for many people the singing of birds is the archetypal sound of spring, there are resonant garden sounds throughout the year, such as the soughing of summer breezes through foliage and the thrashing of tree branches in the equinoctial gales. In Europe, the sweet, sad winter song of the robin always recalls the winter months; while the soothing cooing of pigeons

and doves may be heard year-round in places all over the world. There is also a wide spectrum of rain sounds, from the gentle soft rains of summer showers to the lashing of storms and the brittle reports of sleet and hail, all of them creating different harmonies, depending on whether the rain is falling on leaves, water, clay or wooden tiles, or thatch.

Natural sounds can be augmented effectively by semi-natural ones, set off by wind or water. While Aeolian harps are not to the taste of many gardeners, oriental deer-scarers are increasing in popularity. This device consists of a poised piece of hollow bamboo that, once filled with water, seesaws to empty its load, hitting another piece of wood with a sound like a drumbeat before rebalancing and refilling. Wind chimes may be bought in different pitches in major and minor keys, while among more natural sounds, water has its own repertoire, created by a rill, a fountain, a fall or a spout falling into a still pool.

Do not neglect the resident and visiting insects, birds and small mammals. Listen for the buzz of different kinds of bees, the chirrups of grasshoppers and crickets, and the rattling flight of dragonflies and

LEFT *Lupinus* 'Noble Maiden' is a clump-forming perennial that looks superb when grown informally. Plant two or three as early summer keynotes in a smaller area, to contrast with the colour of other plants such as these oriental poppies (*Papaver orientale*).

ABOVE The bamboo deer-scarer is a means of introducing water in a garden corner too small for a pool or fountain. It works on a simple seesaw principle, the drips filling the hollow cavity until it pivots and drops with a sharp thud on the surrounding pebbles.

large beetles. Sometimes you can hear the cry of a hawk or some other large bird flying over the garden, followed by the sudden disturbance it creates among the smaller birds. Tune your ear to the squeaks of tiny mammals and frogs, and catch the noises of owls and animals that come by night, identifiable only by their highly individual sounds.

VISION AND VISTAS

Glamorous colour photography in magazines and books adds to our knowledge and enjoyment of gardening, but there is a danger of seeing the visual impact of a garden as a flat image on a page and continuing to perceive it in two-dimensional terms.

One of the true pleasures of being inside a garden is being at leisure to walk around it, finding different vistas and focusing on different aspects, both near and far away. You are no longer a remote observer turning the pages of a book, but rather a participator in the garden's sensations, forming your own individual impressions.

It is important when considering one's own garden to maintain a freshness of approach. Without advocating outrageousness for the sake of it, it is still possible to find original combinations of plants and to develop a garden that is wholly individual. Rather than allowing yourself to be dominated by a rigid colour palette, try to aim for a garden that is pleasing to all the senses and all kinds of sensibilities. Letting the design grow out of the nature of the place, rather than from an imposed scheme, gives effects that are likely to be more exciting and satisfying. In such a garden the sights that meet your eye will be a regenerative and lasting source of pleasure.

ABOVE **In this garden good use has been made of interesting near and distant views. The vista, allied with billowing hedges, a linear path that leads into shadow and the splashes of poppy red across the garden in the foreground, give the garden greater dimension.**

DESIGN IN A NATURAL GARDEN

All gardens have an ephemeral quality – change is part of their allure. There are designers who try to limit variation by imposing a severe architectural framework and making the planting conform to strongly disciplined patterns, but in the end all gardens transform themselves with the seasons, the climate and the light, as well as through natural growth and changes in taste.

If you were suddenly to stop all your gardening activity, nature would take over. This could result in your garden declining into a delightful, romantic

place – although it could become a complete mess. Either way, if the garden was left entirely alone, paths would soon become overgrown and impassable and the vegetation would take its own course, moderated only by weather and climate.

While not leaving the garden entirely to nature, there is every advantage in combining its tremendous forces with your own design needs and ambitions. A path to the main door of one's house is a practical convenience, as are sensible boundaries (*see pp.40–41*) and, in consideration of neighbours, a degree of neatness. You will want places to walk and sit in the garden, as well as inviting places to eat and entertain (*see pp.106–109*). You need to consider whether you are a person who prefers sun or shade and how much time you have to work in and enjoy your garden. It is also important to think about the visual impact of the garden from inside your house. You will need to consider the views from different windows and how and when you are going to use the garden. If, for example, you are out at work most of the day, you might consider garden lighting (*see pp.106–109*) and planting in such a way that the best effects are enjoyed early in the morning, as well as at dusk and during darkness. Children or animals who use the garden may also make a difference to your design requirements (*see pp.130–139*).

ABOVE **A fallen birch decays quickly, providing a valuable habitat for a range of microfauna and flora. The open hazel coppice beyond has a typical spring flora of red campion and bluebells.**

RIGHT **Naturalistic borders give a sense of secluded privacy to an urban garden, with osteospermum (*Dimorphotheca pluvialis*) 'Glistening White', blue campanulas, eryngiums, pink hardy geraniums and greater quaking grass (*Briza maxima*).**

NATURAL HABITATS

Achieving variety within a natural style of gardening depends on developing parts of a garden, with a tendency towards a particular condition into a mature habitat. Such places might include: a bank; a dip; a ditch; dry, damp, stony, sunny or shaded ground; or the presence of wild flowers or weeds. The aspect should also be taken into account.

KEY

1 Woodland edge – shade and damp for creatures who shun the sun. Include evergreens. Nectar-rich flowers and bulbs for insects and seeds for birds

2 Lawn – good for birds such as the thrush family and wagtails to forage in. Supports its own special flora – daisies, plantains, speedwells. Site bird baths in the open, on a lawn

3 Meadows and areas of longer grass provide shelter for small mammals and flowers, and seeds for insects and invertebrates, especially butterflies
3a Spring meadow
3b Summer meadow

4 Ponds and bird baths for birds and small mammals to bathe in and drink from

5 Hot dry beds have their own range of plants, many of them with plentiful nectar and pollen, and good seedheads to feed birds and insects

6 Hedges are effective windbreaks and provide shelter for birds in winter and places for them to nest. There may also be flowers and berries

7 Climbing plants give shelter to birds and invertebrates (especially for hibernation) and nesting sites for some birds, such as flycatchers and wrens. They also provide flowers, fruits and seeds

8 Paths and walls contain niches in which rock plants and plants that like dry conditions will grow. Good for invertebrates; small birds nest in suitable holes

9 Trees provide shelter and food and nesting places for resident and visiting birds and insects. In gardens frequented by cats, a hanging bird table, suspended from a branch, is usually the safest type. Trees with deeply furrowed bark are excellent for invertebrates and lichens

10 Log and leaf piles give shelter to beetles and small mammals

11 Sunny bank

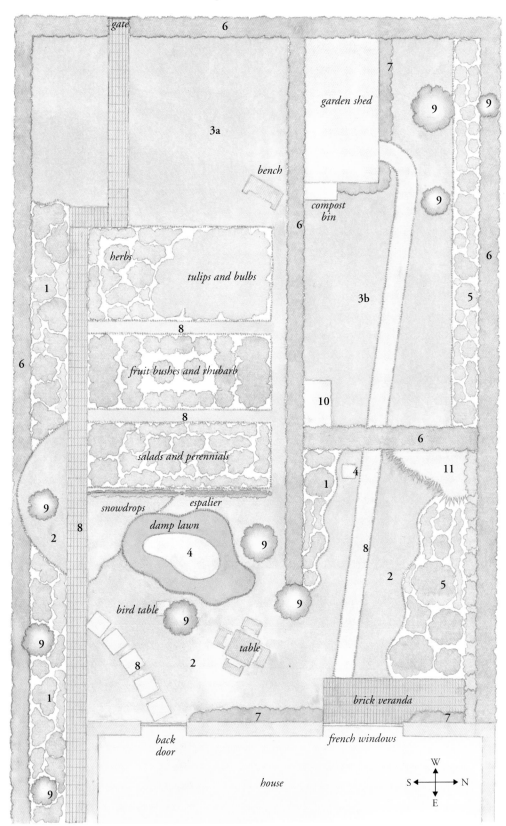

In the end the garden is an individual response that takes into account your needs, ambitions and the kind of management you are prepared to undertake. If you are relaxed about the design and select plants that suit you in both size and form, you will need to do less pruning and general cutting back. If you match those plants to the places that suit them best, they will grow well and not need worrying about. Healthy plants are always a joy and it is worth keeping in mind that quite common plants, in an attractive arrangement and glowing with health, look far better than struggling specialities that are unhappy with their situation. However much you know about gardening, keeping the soil in good condition is always the first consideration, although tackled in a natural way this need not be too great a chore (*see pp.142–145*).

MODELLING FROM NATURE

Even in the best gardens, many of the most beautiful effects happen by chance. The true art of the garden is to recognize and value these fortunate effects that may have been brought about by self-seeding or a particular habit of growth, or by an association of colour, texture or scent that strikes home. I grew up in a garden where, as spring turned to summer, there was an unbelievable haze of blue, as English bluebells and naturalized American larkspur burst into bloom, filling the beds and spilling over on to the path and the driveway. I now believe that a nicely judged association of native and naturalized plants, growing in a harmonious relationship with good planning and design, is one of the most rewarding as well as one of the most easily manageable styles of gardening.

First, however, there needs to be a framework within which the garden can develop. For a garden that takes its cue from the natural world, there is no better model than the natural habitats that are being emulated. Notice plants that grow in drifts – they include many woodlanders, such as erythroniums. You will find that other plants, such as wood anemones and hepaticas, grow in smaller groups,

BELOW **A hot-climate rock garden dominated by dark-leaved, star-like agaves, by lachenalia, with its succulent strappy leaves and ruby-red flowers, as well as a selection of low-growing sedums and sempervivums.**

OPPOSITE **A simple and beautiful combination of** *Erythronium revolutum* **and the elegant shuttlecock fern** *Matteuccia struthiopteris*. **Both will naturalize if they are planted in congenial spots in moist humus-rich soil, in dappled shade.**

A swathe of close-cropped grass next to a drift of meadow flowers and grasses also creates a sense of natural wildness being brought under orderly control. Simply mowing paths through plain grass creates a lovely contrast in colour and texture and is inviting at any time of year.

Even a small garden should have one or two places to sit where you can enjoy sunshine or shade, depending on the time of year and the climate, from where you can see some special vista or feature of the garden. Sitting in the shelter of trees, you can quietly watch the birds at a bird table, look reflectively over a pool or enjoy a vista to a favourite sculpture, fountain or stream.

THEORY INTO PRACTICE

Assessing your garden for the kinds of habitat it contains, and for the prevalent weather and climate conditions, will give you an idea of what will grow. If you put a grid together with your ideas about how the garden will be used by you and your family, while at the same time taking into account the period and size of your house and its immediate surroundings, you will have a rational base on which to build your design. A flowing design, where one part of the garden makes the transition harmoniously into another, gives a sense of natural style.

Many gardens, especially those in urban areas, are longer than they are wide, although the effect can be mitigated by making use of a design that employs lateral sweeps. An espalier of fruit trees is a good way of making a light but definite line across a garden and may be used to mark the end of a wildflower lawn or as a backdrop to a pool. A well-placed artefact, such as a sculpture or a bird bath, can draw the eye, and the surrounding vegetation seems automatically to fall into a composition around it.

Some people like to draw everything out on squared paper, but this is only a good idea at a very early stage. It is far better to get out in the garden, experiencing its full dimensions and judging at first-hand its widths and heights. I like either to stick bamboos into the ground vertically or to lay them on the ground, with a hosepipe mimicking the curves to get an idea of how the intended design will actually use a space. I then look at this crude bamboo/hosepipe artefact, trying to see what the proposed design will look like from every possible angle through the seasons, while making adjustments according to light and shade, space, and the view from different parts of the house and garden.

ABOVE **Closely mown paths wind their way through this meadow garden with its occasional trees. The spring flush is over, leaving the ground to meadow buttercup and flowering grasses. Mowing all over in late summer will leave it neat until the spring flowers start to come up.**

while plants such as lilies are naturally dotted about in ones and twos, and meadow plants grow patchily interwoven in a rich tapestry.

Larger plants play an important role. Trees and shrubs can be brought into prominence at the end of a vista, to punctuate a long border or signal a transition from one habitat to another. Equally, hedges and arbours give height to specific areas of the garden and may be used to create a naturalistic boundary or to divide sections of the garden. If heights are varied, you can create a grassy area with a pleasantly wild feel inside a neater overall design, for example by clipping a hedge at waist height so that you can see over it to the garden beyond. During the less attractive period before mowing, while the flowers are fading and seeding, they will be hidden from view, but when they are in their full glory you will have a treasured area of secret garden.

LEFT *Saponaria ocymoides* has small, slightly irregular flowers. It grows naturally in rocky terrain, but readily takes to growing in dry beds or on walls, where its spreading pink mats are attractive to butterflies.

BELOW *Clematis montana*, in white or pink, is invaluable for north-facing walls and hedges or for growing into big trees. Vigorous and virtually trouble-free, it blooms in spring. Some clematis cultivars are scented.

Trees and shrubs are underused in gardens. Evergreens emerge and come into their own in winter, then melt into the background during spring and summer. Trees in a lawn are always significant, while trees or climbing shrubs, making or draping across archways, create a tantalizing glimpse into another part of a garden. You can also use dainty trees (such as birches) to filter the gaze to another part of the garden.

Always make pathways wider than you think you will require; plants invariably sprawl over them and narrow them considerably. Remember also that, however carefully and beautifully you plan and make your paths, people will always take the direct route to your door, even – sometimes, it seems, especially – if your path goes a different way. Do not try to be too clever – the simplest designs are usually the most effective. As long as you give your garden a good underlying structure that will make the most of its soil conditions and aspect, you can supply all the necessary drama and detail with the plants.

MANAGEMENT

The natural style of gardening should involve a minimum of labour. If hardy plants are chosen and grown in the ground in which they thrive, there should be no need for much interference. On principle, I believe in seeing how plants develop on their own, assuming their mature shapes. This tends to make for a relaxed, interesting kind of garden, although it also involves an element of risk (however, this is true of all kinds of gardening). I will try to match a plant to a place where it will thrive and be an asset to the garden, but if I have made a misjudgment and it does not do well, on the whole, I am prepared

ABOVE **This part of the garden is designed to capture the view to the sea; clipped conifers and neat hedges provide a perfect foil to the natural mixture of foxgloves, grasses, and the oriental poppy; sedum, which is just about to flower, is given a backdrop by the pretty foliage of pittosporum to the right.**

to let it go. Occasionally I may transplant, but gardening for me is a matter of practicalities as well as principle. My gardening time, like that of most people, is limited by the demands of a busy life, leaving no time for complicated techniques or plants that require constant care. This entails having a well-structed garden that can be left untended if I am away or very busy – and then brought back into good fettle with a minimum of work. In general, I aim for effects that can be maintained by the odd half-hour here and there, and I try to make these short bursts of upkeep a pleasure. If you design a garden that is more complicated and demanding than you can easily manage, looking after it turns into a chore and the garden itself becomes a constant reproach.

Thinking time is important. Consider what you are going to plant and where. Taking care with the planting itself is also well worthwhile. Container plants benefit from having at least some of the

pot-peat gently washed or shaken off. As roots can be easily damaged, the plant should then be placed straight into the planting hole, which should always be larger than the extent of the roots. In this way the plants can be safely accommodated and the roots packed in and firmed with good-quality soil. I like to water my plants with a diluted solution of seaweed, as this has a beneficial effect on root growth and helps to minimize the trauma that accompanies transplanting. However, once the plant has settled in I will only water if there are exceptionally high temperatures or in an emergency.

OPPOSITE **The fruits of this hybrid crab apple, 'Red Sentinel', are unpalatable to birds. A dwarf form of apple, a species crab or a rowan attracts a host of birds and insects. A bird bath is a real boon for birds; ideally it should be at least 60cm (2ft) high and sited in an open area.**

USING NATURAL MATERIALS

The twentieth century has brought us many excellent synthetic materials, but in a garden directed towards a natural style authentic materials tend to be more suitable and to weather more satisfactorily than man-made counterparts. Stone, wood, brick and terracotta are all tried and true basic materials that have been used in the garden for centuries. Natural materials generally look more at home in an outdoor situation but they need to be matched sympathetically with the house, the planting and the immediate landscape. Although these materials are beautiful in themselves, it is still important to use them in a way that best exploits their beauty, and to consider a range of design possibilities and combinations.

Natural materials tend to be expensive. If cost is a problem, I would always advise using less of a good quality material rather than large quantities of something inferior. You can always add to a good base, relishing every stage, while a compromise usually remains just that and is often costly to replace. In any case, expense need not be punishing if you spread it out over a period of time. It is a good idea to keep an eye open for local builders' yards, as well as for house clearances, where you stand a good chance of getting some exciting and genuine garden materials at economical prices.

Another means of getting interesting results for a minimal outlay is to mix materials. A few good flagstones that do not quite cover an area can be augmented with bricks to good effect. Flints that infuriate you when you are digging can be used with brick or tile to make a wall that is more interesting than one made with a single material. Anyone can build a small area of wall or a path and this will prove a special pleasure to them because of the extra effort invested in it. With larger projects, it is better to hire a professional to do skilled work, although by doing most of the preparation and labouring yourself you can keep costs to a minimum.

Out of the vast range of natural materials, some have a special association with gardens, having had a long history of use in paving, walls or artefacts.

LIMESTONE A lovely range of stones, soft in both their colours and textures; they weather to a rounded porosity that supports a wide range of beautifully-coloured lichens (oranges, through yellows, greys, grey-greens and white and black). Use limestone for dry-stone walls, paving, balustrading, sculptures, and containers such as urns. It also makes superb flagged courtyards, although there is little pleasure in a beautiful courtyard that has come to you at the expense of a natural limestone landscape. Also, limestone rarely looks its best in areas where it does not occur naturally. Try to buy recycled paving if you are in a limestone area and consider alternatives if you live in an area with other kinds of regional stone.

RIGHT **Rough-cut wooden planking can be used to traverse a marshy area of the garden. It is simple and totally in keeping with an informal part of the garden, and provides dry footing so that you can admire the plants as they grow up and flower.**

BELOW **A glorious wall, with cut stone around the gateway and rough-hewn stone for the rest of the wall, giving ample foothold for a cascade of red and white valerian, as well as ideal niches for** *Campanula poscharskyana* **and red poppies.**

SANDSTONE A wide range of colours, including greys and yellows. A widespread stone – if you look closely, you can see the tiny compressed particles of sand. The fact that it can be crumbly or flaky does not detract from its appeal. It attracts some lichen growth (mainly greeny yellows, greys and brown-blacks, plus some orange leafy lichen on upper faces) and it looks nice with ferns. Use sandstone for walls, which will look glorious with plants growing over them, as well as for paving and sculpture.

GRANITE This hard-wearing, sparkling rock is nicer left rough or semi-polished rather than mirror-polished. Use rough boulders for edging informal paths. Granite attracts interesting lichens in areas of clean air. It comes in reds, pinks, blues and green-greys. Often used in the form of small rectangular setts in the garden, it can be cold, but grass delineation between the setts looks very attractive.

FLINT Large and small flints turn up all the time during the digging of clay-with-flints soils. Use the largest flints for marking out verges. Smaller flints look very handsome incorporated with red brick into walls. Knapped into regular shapes to show a shiny grey-blue or black inner surface, they can be used to make a regular patterning in walls.

SLATE This elegant stone comes in colours from charcoal to a beautiful, blue-grey or muddy pink. It is especially attractive used as flagging in sunny areas, particularly when edged with brick for contrast. It will grow glorious crustose lichens in pastel colours in clean air, giving the stone the appearance of a New England patchwork quilt. Slate can also be used as a table top or bench top.

WOOD Ideal for bench seats with stone, brick or wood supports. Some wooden furniture is tough enough to be left outdoors and will weather nicely.

ABOVE **A hilly woodland walk, with steps held secure by pine trunks wrapped with wire mesh to prevent their becoming slippery. The dark foliage of ferns and shrubs is lit up by lilies, garden columbines (*Aquilegia*), Welsh poppies (*Meconopsis cambrica*), rhododendrons and bugle (*Ajuga reptans*).**

ABOVE LEFT A stone wall in summer, generously colonized with navelwort (*Umbilicus rupestris*), with its flat round leaves and small turrets of green flowers; ivy-leaved toadflax (*Cymbalaria muralis*), dotted with tiny purple and cream snapdragons; and the fern, maidenhair spleenwort (*Asplenium trichomanes*).

ABOVE RIGHT A water sculpture in Monterey, California, made in the trunk of an old tree. Water falls from metal bowls fitted into the crevices, and splashes into a pool at the base. The sculptor, Daryl Stokes, makes similar falls with large pieces of driftwood.

(Check that exotic hardwoods come from managed forests.) Logs make informal steps if wrapped in chicken wire and pegged firmly in place with securely set wooden pegs. They may also be used as sides for retaining walls and raised beds. Decking made from boarding is like a detached veranda, set above ground level on posts and joists. Alternatively, boards can be laid straight into the ground or into gravel. Thoroughly treat with wood preservative. In wet weather the boards are less slippery if wrapped once in chicken wire (although they do not look as nice). White-painted picket fences and gates will give a cottage-garden-style look.

BRICK Lovely for paths and walls. Use with flints or paving to soften hard materials and colours. Lay brick paving over a base of compacted hardcore with a layer of sand smoothed level. Use mortar or butt the bricks together (allowing plants to grow between), depending on the desired effect. Lay the bricks in a neat pattern – a little research may reveal a local brick-laying style, such as herringbone, basketweave or running bond. Alternatively, use repeated groupings of two (or three) laid one way and the same number laid at right angles. Use hard bricks for paths that take a lot of use, and intersperse them at intervals with hard, matt grey stable bricks for effect. Be careful with the match; yellow and grey bricks can look distinctly odd in a red-brick region. Architectural yards can be a good source of second-hand bricks, but make sure they are suitable for the use you have in mind for them.

TERRACOTTA Meaning literally 'baked earth', terracotta is used for roof tiles (tiled sheds and outhouses are very attractive), chimney pots (old ones are often used for plants) and, of course, for plant pots. The architect Edwin Lutyens used tiles on their sides sunk into the ground, together with paving to give texture. Terracotta pots can be used to soften a paved courtyard of stone or composite stone or in paths and steps.

CAST IRON, WROUGHT IRON Cast-iron garden furniture and fittings were the vogue in the nineteenth century, when the process was new. Cast-iron garden benches in the old fern or vine Coalbrookdale designs can still be bought, either new or as antiques. They last as long as their aluminium counterparts but are much heavier. Wrought iron was typically used for making gates, railings and balustrades. Iron fixtures look extemely attractive with plants – either annuals such as sweet peas or a perennial climber such as Japanese wineberry – weaving through the ribs.

COBBLES, GRAVEL, PEBBLES These should be used sparingly to match with the house textures and colours, as well as with the immediate environment. Although they can be a bit of a cliché, they look attractive in a sympathetic setting. Pebble paths are lovely in seaside gardens. The Portuguese made an art of mosaic pebble courtyards and paths. Pebble beaches around water features will look natural as long as they blend in with the surroundings, while pebble pools are safe for children (*see p.139*).

HOW TO MAKE A TURF SEAT

Herb seats date back to the Middle Ages, but are useful and inviting in modern gardens. They consist of a support in brick or stone (rectangular open-topped box of bench size and proportions) almost filled with hardcore, then topped with a layer of soil that is planted with herbs, such as chamomile, thyme, or even lawn turf, planted with daisies. Seat backs and arms can be added if desired.

1 When you have decided on a site for your seat, dig foundations 30cm (12in) deep – a little wider than the wall that will be built on top of it. Fill the trench with hard-core (broken bricks, tiles and stones) and concrete it over, so that it is smooth and level with the ground.

2 Build a brick or stone box over the foundations up to the height you want. Fill the box with hard-core, then small stones and grit (to stop soil particles being washed down into the hard-core), before filling the top 24–30cm (9–12in) with topsoil.

3 Smooth and firm the surface of the soil and lay turf, or plant with chamomile plants, about 7cm (2½in) apart. Sit on it when the plants have become established (see the finished seat on the right). Do not forget to water during dry spells. Trim the plants with hand shears as necessary.

RIGHT This herb seat at Sissinghurst (nicknamed 'Edward the Confessor's chair') was built by Harold Nicolson and Vita Sackville-West's chauffeur with bits of masonry from the old house at Sissinghurst. It is planted with the non-flowering chamomile 'Treneague', with thyme in the paving stones round about and daphne and foxglove to the side.

SPECIAL CONDITIONS

The broad groups of habitat described so far may be found or created in most gardens. Some places, however, have special conditions that would be difficult or impossible to replicate elsewhere. If you are after a conventional kind of garden, with ubiquitous-style beds, borders and a standard hedge, these conditions may seem to be a severe impediment. If, however, you opt for a natural approach and look into the possibilities, you will be able to create a garden that is just as beautiful but has a style of its own and is also easier to care for. The elegant grass gardens of parts of the coastal USA are good examples of this type of garden. In Britain, the celebrated gardener Beth Chatto, at the outset of her gardening career, almost despaired of a dry scorched part of her garden, where as she recalls, 'even native weeds perished'. She therefore decided to borrow from both Mediterranean and American gardens, as well as from natural habitats, and now her dry gardens are world famous.

COASTAL GARDENS

Seaside gardens are among the most beautiful anywhere, although gardening books generally present them as problem cases. This is because salt-laden winds make it especially difficult for inland plants to survive in them. Obviously it would be a mistake to try and make an inland garden on a coastal spit or a woody, rocky cliff edge, and there are certainly preferable alternatives.

One of the most effective, simple gardens I have seen is on the windswept Suffolk coast in eastern England. This area is notorious for its harsh weather conditions and the owners also have to contend with high tides bringing the sea and its detritus to the gate and sometimes into the garden. However, instead of getting rid of the pebbles, the owners have imported more of them from the beach and planted coastal horned poppies (*Glaucium flavum*) and sea kale (*Crambe maritima*) on the shingle, and sea lavender (*Limonium vulgare*) in a pocket of soil. A hebe is enjoying the mild conditions that usually go with a maritime location. There is also *Erigeron* 'Charity', with its pink daisy-like flowers, mounds of silver santolina and sea holly (*Eryngium*). Above the low pebble wall, tamarisk trees (*Tamarix gallica*), flowering crimson and pale peach, are used to break the force of the wind, while wild roses offer a second line of defence.

Even a garden that is practically all rock can be made beautiful by the encouragement of native rock plants and the addition of extra species. Small pockets of soil, given extra humus, will make a naturalistic bed. Depressions in the rock, given some soil, can be planted with salt-tolerant species, such as pink and red varieties of sea thrift (*Armeria alliacea*), vivid blue squills, including spring squill (*Scilla verna*) and autumn squill (*S. autumnalis*), trailing plants such as soapwort (*Saponaria ocymoides*) and

BELOW **A shaded north-facing border, backed by a holly hedge, is given dynamic from the textures of the feathery fennel foliage (*Foeniculum vulgare*), the spear leaves of *Iris orientalis*, and the mounded clumps of flowering *Geranium phaeum* and *Brunnera macrophylla*.**

OPPOSITE **A glorious view across a bay is here seen through an informal grouping of borage (*Borago officinalis*), pot marigold (*Calendula officinalis*), dog daisy (*Leucanthemum vulgare*) and fennel (*Foeniculum vulgare*).**

humps of sea campion (*Silene maritima*). Areas that catch the sunshine will gain extra warmth from the hot rock, permitting hot-climate species to grow, while partly damp shady places will support ferns.

WINDY PLACES

As the owners of homes on moors and high plateaux can testify, it is not only coastal gardens that catch the wind. In such places one can choose a spare, totally natural effect that takes its cue from the surrounding landscape, with few additions, using locally native rock and vegetation to good effect. Alternatively, boundary walls and hedges may be given additional depth (although the young trees may need artificial protection in the form of thick netting or fencing to get them started). Trees and shrubs make the best kind of windbreak, filtering the wind and slowing and softening it. Sycamore (*Acer pseudoplatanus*) will survive very strong, cold winds, while also good are European ash (*Fraxinus excelsior*), white willow (*Salix alba*) and alders, such as *Alnus incana* or *A. rugosa*. In mild areas you can indulge in plants such as golden trumpet tree (*Tabebuia chrysotricha*), Californian laurel (*Umbellularia californica*) and cordylines (*Cordyline australis*). Once a fairly dense windbreak is in place, the garden within will be warmer and more humid and capable of playing host to a wider range of plants. The bright *Geranium sanguineum*, the silvery artemisia (*Artemisia absinthium* 'Lambrook Silver') and cone flower (*Echinacea purpurea*) are among those plants that stand up well to windy conditions.

PROTECTION FROM POLLUTION

Windbreaks are invaluable in noisy, polluted, urban areas. Larger gardens can be protected from both fumes and traffic noise by an informal break of trees and shrubs planted two or three deep. A good thick hedge will do a lot to bring peace to a smaller garden. There is a wide range of plants that tolerate a certain level of pollution, including laburnums (*Laburnum*), robinia (*Robinia pseudoacacia*), the Japanese quinces (*Chaenomeles*) and European and North American amelanchiers. Other shrubs include *Philadelphus*, cotoneasters, privet, spiraeas and *Buddleja davidii*.

LEFT Heather growing as it should, in a natural way, in a sandy, heathy landscape with scattered trees. This particular species of heather is *Erica* x *darleyensis* 'Margaret Porter', which flowers in late winter and early spring.

Climbing plants that also tolerate polluted air include the scarlet *Campsis radicans* and the charming, partly self-supporting climbing hydrangea, *Hydrangea anomala petiolaris*. There is a large number of perennial plants to choose from, including the large-leaved *Bergenia cordifolia*, the dainty *Dicentra eximia,* and *D. formosa, Euphorbia amygdaloides* and *Smilacina racemosa*, as well as most of the rudbeckias, symphytums and thalictrums.

DRY SHADY PLACES

Dry shade is considered one of the worst situations for any garden, although there are many plants that will tolerate this condition. Among the shrubs are the green-flowered scented *Daphne laureola*, holly (*Ilex aquifolium*) and dwarf cornel (*Cornus canadensis*), as well as the shiny-leaved, prostrate evergreen *Rubus tricolor*. Climbers such as Boston ivy (*Parthenocissus tricuspidata*) and *Euonymus fortunei* and its many variants tolerate dry shade, as do many perennials, such as the dicentras, *Iris foetidissima, Symphytum grandiflorum, Vinca minor* and, for large areas, the tough, purple-to-white *Trachystemon orientalis*.

SWEET SOILS – CHALK LIMESTONE

I have always loved the characteristic flora of chalk and limestone, and since I have never been an admirer of azaleas, rhododendrons or heathers, I do not in the least miss those species that are not lime-tolerant. For gardeners who like the heath family, winter heath (*Erica carnea*), Corsican heath (*E. terminalis*) and *E.* x *darleyensis* will all grow in alkaline soils. Many of the most beautiful European wildflowers, such as Pasque flowers and most hellebores, are found on sweet alkaline soils, while the limestone mountains of southern Europe have a spectacular and interesting floral repertoire that includes many of our culinary herbs. Limestone base soils and rocks are also found in the United States, as well as throughout Asia.

ACIDIC SOILS

Gardens on an acid base rock such as granite or basalt, or with very peaty ground, have acid soils that support a diverse flora from all parts of the world – not only a truly vast range of heathers and rhododendrons, but also many of the lily family, most gentians, and some splendid trees, such as magnolias and enkianthus. Dry acid soils are sometimes perceived as a problem, but even here there are many plants that do well: the broom family (*Cytisus*), bushy sun roses (*Cistus*), indigoferas, and individuals, such as *Rosa pimpinellifolia* and the Australasian *Hakea microcarpa*, which makes a large dense shrub with scented, creamy flowers. Holly trees (*Ilex*), birches (*Betula*) and aspen (*Populus alba tremula*) also tolerate such extreme conditions.

HEATHLANDS

Although heaths and moorlands in their natural state are open, uncultivated kinds of land with a typically acidic soil, this does not mean they are devoid of plants. Whether we refer to sandy lowland types of heath or the damp heather moors of high ground, there are plants that thrive in these conditions, augmented (especially in the case of heathers) by the introduction of many cultivars. There are also delightful plants, such as harebells (*Campanula rotundifolia*) and mulleins (*Verbascum*) for sandy conditions, and the dainty *Linnaea borealis*, found in both Eurasia and North America (for damp peaty soils). Trees include birches and Scots pine (*Pinus sylvestris*). Heathers are plants from Eurasia and of temperate Africa, although, interestingly, one of the most beautifully natural-looking heather gardens I have come across was in northern California.

BELOW The lesser periwinkle (*Vinca minor*) is one of the nicest species in a very useful genus. It will tuck itself into dark dry corners and, once established, makes a lovely glossy-leaved mat sparkling with small flowers – this is the white form, *Vinca minor* f. *alba*.

THE NATURAL ORDER

It may sound like a contradiction in terms to maintain a natural style, but there is no room for illusion. All gardening requires some management, and each of the habitats you are working with will need to be kept in trim, in order to maintain its characteristic natural appearance. Wildflower lawns and summer meadows need mowing at intervals that will allow the plants their best opportunities. Walls need to have their basic condition maintained and plants that are perhaps becoming overgrown may have to be checked. Extremely vigorous plants may need restraint in a woodland or prairie setting, before they start to overwhelm their neighbours. Some of the more vigorous water and waterside plants usually need some attention at the end of the year, and it is wise at the same time to check over your pool for general health and to neaten it up so that it continues to look attractive even when the plants are dormant in winter. Even vegetables that are easy to grow need some tending, especially in the early stages, and fruit trees generally benefit from some pruning, even if it is only occasional.

FLEXIBLE DESIGN

If you are happy with a garden based upon natural models, you should be prepared to some extent to go with the flow of the plants you have chosen, and adapt your original design year by year as the plants grow and mature, spread, and self-seed. It is likely that a newly laid brick or flagstone courtyard or small terrace will soon start to show plant life in the cracks and crevices. You may even have encouraged this by sweeping seeds across it or by planting suitable subjects such as thyme. Unfortunately, unsuitable plants that you will have no wish to encourage will also start appearing. As few people would want a terrace grown over with dandelions or sprinkled with weedy annuals, some editing of your natural growth will have to take place. A weeding knife, especially designed for this purpose, is the handiest tool for the job.

It is a good rule not to pull out any plants that you cannot identify. You never know what seeds may have floated in on the wind or been brought by the birds, which then found a suitable place in a new habitat that you have developed. Several favourite plants in my garden have arrived by natural means, including the shade-loving *Geranium nodosum* (whose seeds must have come from the south of France on car wheels or clothes) and a *Corydalis ochroleuca* that first took up its abode on my small south-facing brick terrace and has since spread to other locations in the garden.

In my experience, plants that have self-seeded are generally speaking not only more likely to survive but are often slightly healthier than those you have introduced yourself. This is because the plant sheds its seed at the right time after it has found its correct niche in the garden environment. Plants, of course, have no sense of overall design, but I have often been surprised and delighted by the beautiful effects made by plants that have sown themselves.

BELOW Even natural stone can have a harsh colouration, calling out for flower and foliage. Here, a shallow flight of steps has become a rock garden, with thymes of different kinds, *Acaena microphylla*, violets and other rock plants.

Undesirable annual and perennial weeds will need removing as in any garden, but if you take them up before they seed, you can put most of them on the compost heap. I would never recommend putting the roots of couch (*Elymus repens*), dandelion (*Taraxacum*), dock (*Rumex*) or bindweed (*Calystegia/Convulvulus*) into the compost process, although I always tear away the leaves and stems for the compost bin (except for bindweeds which can grow from small parts of stem). Dock roots actually contain chemical inhibitors that protect them from the normal decaying processes of soil bacteria and soil fungi. The long tap roots of dock and dandelion are full of minerals from the ground, which it would be a shame to lose. The separated roots can be thrown away or put into a bin bag and left for at least a year to make a garden silage that can then be added to the compost. They decompose faster if they are left in the sun for a day and then cut or broken up. Do not, however, cut or break them in the ground if you can possibly help it. If you rotavate a dandelion and dock patch, for example, it looks fine for a month or two, but each small cut section of root can grow, like the broom of the Sorcerer's Apprentice, to make a new plant.

WEED CHECKLIST

● Enjoy your garden and try to spend a few minutes each day out there. If you remove a few weeds here and there each time, you will keep on top of the situation.

● Do not let weeds flower and seed. If you have no time to weed thoroughly, at least tear the flowerheads off. You can put most pre-flowering annual weeds and many perennials directly into the compost bins, where they will provide an excellent nutrient input.

● Use the weeds as a soil-type indicator.

● Remember weeds, like all plants, need light to grow – covering the ground will inhibit them. Some commercially available black plastic sheetings are perforated to allow some water through.

● Enjoy your weeds. Watch out for new species. Learn the pleasures of drawing out a metre-long (3ft) white-fanged couch rhizome or a line-up of linked creeping buttercups.

● Consume as many of your (edible) weeds as you can. Nothing inhibits a weed so much as being turned into a crop. Chickweed, ground elder and dandelion are all tasty. However, only eat those that you are certain are nutritious. Remember that weeds such as corn cockle and ragwort are poisonous, while others can cause skin irritation, rashes or blistering. It is always wise to wear gloves and sensible shoes and trousers when weeding.

ABOVE **An enchanting mixture of the neat and the untamed, with the fruit trees and elder allowed their natural shapes and the herb foliage billowing below; the grass has been mown short and the paths and bed edges are scrupulously neat.**

PRECAUTIONARY PRINCIPLES

It is inconceivable that one or two individual gardeners could be held responsible for the rampaging colonization of alien plants over an important natural habitat, following the introduction of new species. In every case where this has happened, to my knowledge, it has resulted from widespread introduction into gardens, or even officially sanctioned introductions into the wild on a large scale which have unfortunately got out of hand. For example, mesembryanthemum, or ice plant (*Caprobrotus edule*), was planted to stabilize Californian roadcuts, but then began to encroach severely on native sand-dunes and coastal scrub vegetation. The common aquatic plant, water hyacinth (*Eichhornia crassipes*), indigenous to tropical America, was introduced as an ornamental to water systems but spread to choke waterways in many parts of the world. In Indonesia, it has, however, begun to be harvested as a food for pigs.

Another nuisance, Japanese knotweed (*Fallopia japonica*) has spread dramatically in Great Britain. It is known to have been introduced from a nursery in The Netherlands, and it naturalized itself; it has been known in the wild for over a hundred years. Himalayan balsam (*Impatiens balsamifera*), introduced as a garden plant, naturalized readily in both Europe and North America, and has become an aggressive colonizer along slow-moving waterways in Britain. The vigour of both these plants seems now to be lessening, although population dynamics of naturalized weeds are imperfectly understood. The pondweed *Elodea canadensis*, introduced to the British Isles in 1834 and to New Zealand in the 1870s, rapidly spread to become a pernicious weed, but in its British sites it began to decline in the 1880s, although a related species, *E. nuttallii*, is now taking its place.

Plants that run riot are usually fairly reticent in their native regions. The beautiful, scented *Rosa eglanteria* is not especially common in its native Europe, nor in its naturalized sites in North America, but it is a terrible nuisance in New Zealand, as is the Eurasian native clematis 'old man's beard' (*Clematis vitalba*). The pretty Eurasian waterside plant purple loosestrife (*Lythrum salicaria*) has recently become a problem in parts of North America, especially in the Canadian province of Ontario. Sometimes a plant can become a nuisance locally, as the American journalist Eleanor Perényi found when the attractive star of Bethlehem (*Ornithogalum umbellatum*) took over the lawn of her garden in Stonington, Connecticut. This plant is native to lowland Europe

BELOW **The beautiful waving plumes of miscanthus grass (here growing respectably with teasel (*Dipsacus*) and neat conifers) may be a problem for the future. In hot dry regions of the USA it is beginning to self-seed outside gardens in open countryside, and there are fears that it may overwhelm native plants.**

and has naturalized unobtrusively in parts of England. Chincherinchee (*O. thrysoides*) from South Africa is a garden ornamental that ventures timidly beyond the garden in some places, but is resented as a noxious weed in southern Australia. The flora and fauna of Australia and New Zealand are particularly vulnerable to alien introductions, but the fast-growing eucalyptus trees have exacted vengence in southern Africa, the Mediterranean, East Africa, Sri Lanka and California.

GARDENING GUIDELINES

Naturalization is never straightforward, however. The many species of eucalyptus trees that dominate parts of the Californian landscape, and which are the despair of conservationists concerned for the native ecology, have interwoven themselves into the ecological fabric in parts of the Big Sur. Opposition to an eradication programme has come from the local historical society, because of the age and size of some of the trees, from biologists concerned for the monarch butterflies that use the eucalyptus as a roost as they migrate down the coast, and also from ornithologists, who appreciate the value of the flowers to orioles and yellow-rumped warblers.

The precarious flora of this area of Californian coastline is also colonized by pampas grass (*Cortaderia atacamensis*) – considered by many to pose the most serious threat of all. Once established, it is difficult to eradicate and many residents of the region are still unwittingly planting it in their gardens, from where the seeds blow out into the wild. Another cause of this plant's spread is termed 'honeymoon dispersal mechanism', in recognition of the fashion among newly-weds of attaching a pampas plume to the radio aerials of their cars.

There are no precise rules governing the naturalization of plants. Some have grown strongly in gardens for centuries and never hop over the fence; others make a break for it during periods of social, horticultural or climatic change; for others there is as yet no satisfactory explanation for their erratic behaviour. It is, however, possible to outline a sensible code of practice for gardeners. In various places throughout the world it is actually illegal to import or plant certain species, although being in touch with a local wildlife centre would raise awareness in a neighbourhood or region well before legislation was enacted and might help halt the spread of nuisance plants. In the case of water plants, it is particularly important never to dump surplus plant material into the local waterways; much better to put it onto the compost heap, where it can be recycled back into the garden without causing harm.

Keeping a wary eye on changes in your local landscape and reporting unusual changes in plant life can also help to keep regional ecologists informed on the overall state of the flora. Even with every precaution, there will still be changes. Fauna and flora exists in a continual dynamic – sometimes in equilibrium, sometimes in violent change. There is no possible way we can put a hold on history but, as natural gardeners, we can at least try not to be environmental vandals.

ABOVE LEFT **Russian vine** (*Fallopia baldschuanica*) grows prodigiously, although, as yet, it shows no sign of becoming rampant in the countryside. Plants in the wild are widespread but scattered, almost always taking root from specimens that gardens have discarded, or on the sites of derelict gardens.

ABOVE RIGHT **Purple loosestrife** (*Lythrum salicaria*) looks marvellous here in a mixed poolside planting; in the USA, however, it has naturalized so vigorously that conservationists are seriously worried that it may be swamping native wild lakeside and marshland species.

BOUNDARIES

Although the grand landscape style appears to merge individual property with the wider landscape, in fact it only conceals the legal boundaries of property and land use that are everywhere strictly delineated. Gardens require definition and smaller gardens, where properties abut, need clear boundaries. This need not entail conformism; there are many ways of marking boundaries, both living and inorganic.

Walls are usually best made of local materials, and may be ornamented and softened with climbing plants. If you inherit an ugly existing wall, you can probably clothe it in flower and foliage within a short period, thus turning an eyesore into an asset.

Fencing can be carried out in a vast number of materials and styles. For a natural effect, examine the styles of fence and gate in your region and search out something that appeals to you. The great English gardener Gertrude Jekyll observed the styles in her home region and made a fine portfolio of different styles, carried out by local craftsmen. Although mass production dominates nowadays, you may well happen on a craft style or a way of doing things that gives a local signature.

As with fences, you can sometimes happen on local craft styles for gates. Distinct styles of gate, for example, still identify specific localities in southern England. The USA takes pride in its fence styles: split oak and chestnut were used for the zigzag Virginian rail fence and hickory or locust tree in Pennsylvanian post and rail, while Wyoming mitred buck fencing was constructed from local saplings.

HEDGES

Hedges give gardens both a sense of secure enclosure and natural order. They can also open to disclose a view or close off an unsightly prospect. Hedge plants that grow naturally large may be grown as a clipped monoculture – privet, box, yew, beech, hornbeam, and hawthorn, for example. Left to itself a hedge naturally gains other species of plants. My own late-

BELOW **An informal hedge of *Rosa rugosa* is hardy, windproof and fragrant in summer. The semidouble pink-flowered variety 'Belle Poitevine' has rich bushy foliage and so is excellent for hedging. It is also highly scented and will thrive in poor soils.**

nineteenth-century hedges, originally pure hawthorn, have now accrued wild rose, field maple, holly, hazel and oak, as well as ivy and honeysuckle. I find that I only need to give them a light trim twice a year.

Informal hedges take up more room but can be mysterious and relaxing. Rugosa roses and species shrub roses are ideal for informal hedges, together with species such as cotinus (*Cotinus coggygria*), eleagnus (*Eleagnus angustifolia*), cornelian cherry (*Cornus mas*) and viburnum (*Viburnum lantana*). These may be planted in loose groupings or as a mixture of shrubs. One of the most effective is a hedge that starts off with perhaps three or four species, planted slightly unevenly rather than in an exact straight line, and that allows the shrubs to make more or less their natural heights and spreads.

Using different varieties of a single species such as *Rosa rugosa* is better for smaller hedges. Its rich foliage and scented flowers make this one of the most beautiful of all hedging plants, whether planted with, say, all-white varieties or with pink, red and white. Planting in strict sequence will, however, create an undesirable formality, so dot colours here and there.

While hedge plants are getting their roots established and filling out, you may need to put in fencing to create a temporary boundary. This will also have the effect of giving some shelter to the maturing shrubs. When planting, prepare the ground well, as you would for individual trees or shrubs, and loosen the soil around the planting trench or holes; otherwise in heavy soils you may find the roots will be constricted and the excavations may act as a sump, injuring the roots by waterlogging.

INTERNAL DIVISIONS

It is often not appreciated how effective a prickly and spiny hedge is in deterring burglars. Ferocious hedging plants include holly (*Ilex*), *Pyracantha*, *Berberis* and hawthorn (*Crataegus*), although you could choose anything that grows well locally and produces unwelcoming prickles and spines. Choose carefully and make sure you have the right trimming and pruning equipment, as well as thick protective gloves and clothing – it will be you who will be carrying out any necessary maintenance and you will not want to impale yourself. As well as giving definition to the boundaries of your property, internal division may be used to redefine certain areas within the garden. Sometimes dividing a garden a little can create an impression of greater space, although excessive subdivisions are more for a

formal than an informally natural character. You may, for example, choose a hedge to separate a wildflower orchard from a herb garden, perhaps clipping it lower than the outer boundary hedge, while at the same time indicating a clear division. You may use something as simple as a swathe of close-mown grass to separate an area of longer grass from a pathway or rough lawn. A line of espalier fruit trees makes a living trellis that suitably separates off a vegetable- or fruit-growing area. Walls may also be built inside the garden but they need to be used judiciously, as too much hardware will defeat a natural appearance. Internal hedges may be cut high or low, as well as being grown wide or narrow. You can allow yourself to have some fun, planning where to cut gaps, gateways, archways or vistas through them.

ABOVE **A romantic end to a country garden, with a gate nestling under a tree on either side. The picket gate marks a definite boundary and allows not only a view to the outside, but also lets evening sunlight filter through.**

CREATING A NATURAL GARDEN

Making and developing a garden in a natural style is a most creative and pleasurable activity, because it involves a growing harmony with your surroundings and the flow of natural life. Go at your own pace; this enterprise calls for planning your garden with understanding and clarity rather than speed. Even small changes make themselves felt within the larger scheme, and you can gradually build up the composition of the different habitats until you reach a balance of apropriate plants that pleases you. This part of the book takes you through a progression of garden habitats and suggests a number of ways to develop them.

LEFT There are few flowers more beautiful or more indicative of ancient woodland than the wood anemone (*Anemone nemorosa*). In this garden scene the carpet of natural white flowers has been augmented by a small drift of a pink variety.

BENEATH THE TREES

After the dormancy of winter, the freshness and beauty of the early flora of deciduous woodland is one of the glories of the temperate world. In European forests there are wild daffodils (*Narcissus pseudonarcissus*), bluebells (*Hyacinthoides non-scripta*) and wood anemones (*Anemone nemorosa*). In North America there are early phloxes, false spikenard (*Smilacina racemosa*) and dog's-tooth violet (*Erythronium*). While I always try to use native species as a basis for a woodland-edge scheme, a garden can assimilate spring plants from many places, and natives and introductions can be planted together successfully in a natural style. This is an enterprise that needs taste and restraint, for woodlands more than any other habitat begin to look artificial if they become overcrowded. Choosing a few species that do well and encouraging self-seeding will usually work better than trying to cram in too many different kinds of plant.

Along the edges of woods and beside the paths, where more light falls than in the dense interior canopy, a succession of flowers will bloom throughout summer and autumn, and it is from these areas that you can take your cue for the woodland habitat of the garden. The design approach and the kinds and number of species you choose will depend on the size of your garden as well as the scope of your ambition.

At the very minimum you will be able to grow snowdrops (*Galanthus nivalis*) or winter aconite (*Eranthis hyemalis*), dame's violet (*Hesperis matronalis*) and honesty (*Lunaria annua*) along the shady base of a hedge or wall. In a large-scale garden you could also plant some extra trees and make a path that curves through the trees, perhaps to an open clearing.

Many people perceive shade as a disadvantage, but those who already have a self-sustaining shady border, beneath trees or on the cooler side of a hedge, appreciate the beautiful foliage effects and longer, lasting periods of flower. Some of the most subtle and successful effects in the garden can be created within shady borders. As this habitat supports a particularly wide range of plants, there is no shortage of choice, even in early summer. You could perhaps have lily-of-the-valley, originally from mainland Europe, hostas from Japan, and tiarellas (or foam flower) from North America. The arching Solomon's seal has representatives on both side of the Atlantic – such as *Polygonatum odoratum* in Europe and *P. biflorum* in North America. These grow well even in quite dense shade, as can the equally attractive false spikenard, native to much of North America and naturalized throughout Europe and other temperate regions, where it has been able to spread from gardens.

Woodland-edge soil is usually rich and quite fertile, thanks to continual conditioning from layers of natural leaf mould. Shade-loving woodland plants therefore do much better in these fertile conditions than, for example, herbs. If the area you have in mind for a woodland edge has poor soil, foxgloves (*Digitalis*), bluebells and red campion (*Silene dioica*), foam flowers (*Tiarella cordifolia*), cyclamen (*Cyclamen hederifolium* or *C. coum*) and hellebores are all good plants to use as first colonizers while you build up fertility by adding compost and leaf mould.

BELOW **Early spring flowers, such as snowdrops (***Galanthus nivalis***), winter aconites (***Eranthis hyemalis***) and early flowering hellebores, are sturdy enough to withstand sudden snowfall and late frosts. These plants look best under the natural shelter of deciduous shrubs and trees, such as a greening Oregon plum (***Oemleria cerasiformis***).**

OPPOSITE **For a shaded part of the garden, where a woodland-edge habitat can be created, the fresh new foliage of a simple male fern (***Dryopteris filix-mas***) and hart's tongue (***Asplenium scolopendrium***), growing through the purple-tinged, low shoots of ***Rubus***, strike exactly the right note.**

WOODLAND FLORA IN THE GARDEN

The area in most gardens where shade is dominant is usually the best place to start with woodland flora. In a completely new garden you will need to design a shape and provide the total complement of plants, but most of us take on gardens that are already planted and have some affection for some of the existing plants. I feel it is a shame to sacrifice everything to a new principle when you could possibly retain some of the plants that are well established and healthy. The transformation to a more natural style should flow gently, opening out gradually to take on the new design with a mixture of additional plants.

In wild conditions the flower-rich edge of woodland gradually merges into deep forest. As this is unlikely to occur in the garden, you need a distinct framework, perhaps that of the garden boundary itself, which might be a wall or hedge. If your garden lies on an east–west axis there is the opportunity for a north-facing, long woodland-edge border that can be a pure delight. A longish border between a path and a boundary hedge, for example, can have a number of phases, punctuated by taller plants. Such phasing could also be practised in a rectangular or irregular area, such as at the bottom of the garden or in an alcove. When working with a fairly long border, I like to create a sense of pace by interrupting the high border plants with a small grassy area, perhaps with a small tree or trees to give the impression of a linear woodland walk. A group of snowdrops (*Galanthus*),

dog's-tooth violets (*Erythronium*) or autumn crocus (*Colchicum*), planted in the grass, continues the woodland theme, while still allowing for the grassy area to be mown through most of the year, after the bulb foliage has died back.

THROUGH THE SEASONS

Snowdrops and dog's-tooth violets do equally well in beds and borders, along with other very easily established winter-into-spring plants such as cyclamen. Two mainstays are the dainty *Cyclamen hederifolium* and *C. coum* (flowering in autumn and winter respectively), which develop very rapidly from corms and give delightful silver-on-dark-green leaf patterning, as well as attractive pink flowers blotched deep carmine at the mouth. Both species have attractive white forms.

Violets, such as the scented *Viola odorata*, which flowers in spring, and the purplish-leaved *V. labradorica*, which flowers slightly later from spring into early summer, are hardy and easy to establish, while the elegant *V. cornuta*, native to the mountains of the Pyrenees, has been widely adopted as a garden plant and has naturalized. The USA has its own range of wild violets, a few of which are available in Europe, such as the scented *V. canadensis* and the cream-coloured *V. striata*. A patch of the white or pale blue *V. cornuta* looks lovely, but all violas make a valuable contribution, whether planted in groups or dotted about in individual clumps. The idea in this habitat is to make a rich patchwork of woodland species. This could also include wood anemone, widely naturalized all over the world, and cardamines of various kinds, including the very hardy, deep lilac-pink *Cardamine pentaphyllos* and fluffy white *C. trifolia*.

The exquisite erythroniums, known as dog's-tooth violets (though not violets), and trout lilies (though not lilies) have native representatives in North America and Eurasia. Despite their fragile appearance, they will naturalize quite readily in suitable soils. They are quiet plants and look best when planted in small groups, offset against a background of ferns or foliage which show up the full beauty of their spotted glossy leaves and thrown-back flowers.

Brilliant drifts of spring colour give place to pale glimmering blooms that light up the summer shade. Several hardy geraniums thrive in these conditions. The semi-evergreen *Geranium maccrorhizum*, with

BELOW Colchicums (*Colchicum autumnale*) growing in turf. There are fancier varieties, but in a naturalistic planting this species looks superb.

BOTTOM Forget-me-nots (*Mysotis*) line the path to the woodland, presided over by fine foxgloves (*Digitalis purpurea*). Foam flower (*Tiarella cordifolia*) can be seen in the foreground.

its scented leaves, makes an attractive rounded hump of foliage when not flowering. The delightful widow's veil (*G. phaeum*) and the white form of the common herb Robert (*G. robertianum*), which will lighten a dark corner, both self-seed readily. The attractive North American species *G. maculatum* grows best in drifts in moist dappled shade, and *G. sylvaticum* will survive trying conditions.

These geraniums look well grown with taller summer plants, such as foxgloves (*Digitalis purpurea*). The pure white form looks startling in shaded conditions, but both pink and white self-seed naturally and dot themselves about. Also tallish and clumping, astilbes and astrantias shine in the late summer, and the Japanese anemone (*Anemone hupehensis*) is a treasure that once established will flower and increase reliably.

PLANTING PLAN FOR A WOODLAND EDGE

The shaded environment beneath trees can be one of the most beautiful in a garden. Soil that is initially dry and poor can be improved naturally with the introduction of leaf mould or organic compost (a quick route to the rich buildup of humus that occurs in a natural woodland). Woodland plants in this dappled woodland-edge situation bloom well over a long period.

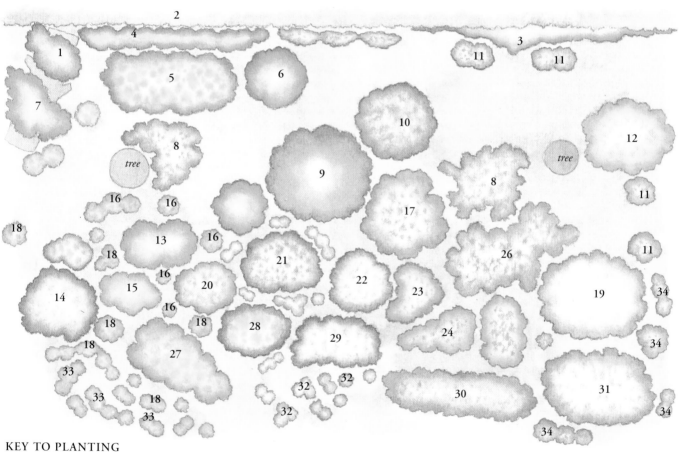

KEY TO PLANTING

1 Ivy *Hedera helix*
2 Beech hedge *Fagus sylvatica*
3 *Clematis montana*
4 Comfrey *Symphytum grandiflorum*
5 Yellow loosestrife *Lysimachia vulgaris*
6 Male fern *Dryopteris filix-mas*
7 Virginia creeper *Parthenocissus quinquefolia*
8 Cyclamen *Cyclamen hederifolium*
9 *Cotinus* 'Grace'
10 Fennel *Foeniculum vulgare* 'Purpureum'
11 Honesty *Lunaria annua*
12 *Geranium macrorrhizum*

13 Hart's-tongue fern *Asplenium scolopenium*
14 *Rubus* 'Benenden'
15 *Tolmiea menziessi* 'Taff's Gold'
16 Welsh poppy *Meconopsis cambrica*
17 Foxglove *Digitalis purpurea*
18 Daffodil *Narcissus pseudo-narcissus* 'Tête-à-tête'
19 Gillenia *Gillenia trifoliata*
20 *Geranium sylvaticum*
21 *Geranium phaeum*
22 Snowy woodrush *Luzula nivea*
23 Sweet woodruff *Galium odoratum*

24 *Cardamine pentaphyllum*
25 American cowslip *Dodecatheon pulchellum*
26 Bluebell *Hyacinthoides hispanica*
27 Lady's mantle *Alchemilla mollis*
28 Dog's-tooth violet/trout lily *Erythronium americanum*
29 *Lamium* 'White Nancy'
30 Bugle *Ajuga reptans* 'Atropurpurea'
31 *Brunnera macrophylla*
32 Snowdrop *Galanthus nivalis*
33 Winter aconite *Eranthis hyemalis*
34 Blue phlox *Phlox divaricata*

SHRUBS AND CLIMBERS

The woodland edge is a place where shrubs thrive because more light is available, in contrast to the inner heartland of the forest. The garden counterpart has immense possibilities and indeed one has to hold back from the temptation to plant too many shrubs (especially when they are young and small) or the woodland edge will become a shrubbery. Placing shrubs at intervals to suit the spirit of your design, giving a flow in terms of colour and texture, however, makes a desirable change of pace. When planning such an area, I look first at the native shrubs of a region, then at other shrubs that perform particularly well in shade and for which I have a preference, and gradually fine-tune a personal choice that suits that particular piece of woodland garden.

Shrubs are particularly useful in punctuating a long shady border. I originally picked out *Rubus* 'Benenden' for its large white flowers, which bloom in spring, but was pleased to find the foliage turns a beautiful amber in late summer. Viburnums have a huge geographical range and make a pleasing ingredient to a woodland-edge border, especially if you can key in the species with those that grow naturally in the surrounding landscape. Wayfaring tree (*Viburnum lantana*) grows along the roadsides near woods not far from where I live, and I chose the similar looking *V. carlesii* 'Diana', which has compact

growth and richly-scented spring flowers. If my border merged into grass rather than a path, I would have planted the guelder rose (*Viburnum opulus*) in the dappled shade, for its beautiful glossy leaves, white lacecap flowers and glorious red berries. There must be a viburnum for nearly every situation, but it is important in natural gardening to choose a kind that fits with both the garden location and the woodland theme.

Indian physic (*Gillenia trifoliata*) is an unusual shrub that rewards close inspection. It has dark, bronzy foliage, its three-lobed leaves growing on red-brown twigs and bears dainty and brilliant irregular white stars, which seem to float against the darker background over a long flowering season. *Gillenia* grows naturally along roadsides near upland woods over a wide area of North America, where it is known as Bowman's root and Indian physic. It takes readily to woodland-edge borders in light shade and to areas where the soil profile tends to be a little more acidic than the rest of a garden, as it can be in places on generally lime-rich ground.

Large shrubs with open foliage, such as *Hydrangea quercifolia*, have a natural feel and look well judiciously placed in larger woodland gardens. However, in general, I feel the large showy exotics such as hydrangeas or rhododendrons should be used with extreme caution as they dominate the garden, striking too strident and artificial a note. Sometimes, however, flora from far afield works very well together with native plants. Sometimes happy associations occur almost accidentally. An instance of this happened in my woodland-edge border, when I decided to plant a bush of *Cotinus* 'Grace', which has large purple-tinged leaves – although I cautiously planted it near the back of my shady border. Behind it, a self-seeded fennel sprang up and to the side a tree paeony (*P. delavayii*, an exotic shrub raised from a cutting), which has rather beautiful, cut-leaved foliage and deep crimson flowers, was beginning to fill out. In between, a self-seeded, dark purple *Geranium phaeum* and some chocolate-coloured columbines (*Aquilegia vulgaris*) made this one of the most attractive parts of the shady wood-edge border, even though it had come together almost by chance.

Golden foliage plants, such as *Robinia pseudacacia* 'Frisia', look extremely unnatural and are used far too much as a quick means of creating a dramatic effect. Some plants, however, have a golden glow that is not

BELOW **Witch hazels (*Hamamelis*) bring their bright wispy flowers and strong scent to late winter and early spring. Lemon-coloured 'Sunburst' grows here with the cultivar 'Diane', which has coppery-coloured flowers. Both bloom from mid- to late winter and require neutral to acidic soil conditions to grow well.**

so flashy and just what is needed at a certain point in planting in shady conditions among trees and shrubs. One perennial I would include in this select group is *Tolmiea menziesii* 'Taff's Gold' as it is not only among the best golden foliage plants but also thrives in shade. It is low-growing and undemanding, with handsome soft foliage speckled with gold. It spreads quietly to make a small, golden-green pool of colour and will grow even in dry deep shade. New plants form on top of the leaves where the old leaf meets the leaf stalk. Tolmieas come originally from western North America, but they seem to fit in happily in shady places in gardens far from home. Bolder and more showy, *Hosta* 'Midas Gold' is a golden form that does well in shade, while the discreet golden form of creeping Jenny (*Lysimachia nummularia* 'Aurea') will run prettily under trees and shrubs in light to medium shade. I am tempted also

by *Rubus idaeus* 'Aureus', which makes a small glowing bush in lightly shaded conditions. Place the golden plants sparingly and separate them by others with darker foliage. Allow the yellow or golden forms of the Welsh poppy (*Mecanopsis cambrica*) to self-seed and any prejudice you may have held against these sometimes garish plants will be replaced with real appreciation.

CLIMBING PLANTS

Well-chosen climbing plants bring an airy lightness of flower to the trees or hedges they drape, and lead the eye upwards. They can be combined with shrubs in a woodland-edge context: I look out onto my woodland border through a window framed with Mexican orange blossom (*Choisiya ternata*) on one side and the partly evergreen winter fragrant honeysuckle (*Lonicera fragrantissima*) on the other.

ABOVE **Mock orange (*Philadelphus*) makes a lovely garden shrub, with its rich scent and white flowers. There are single- and double-flowered cultivars. 'Belle Etoile', with a crimson dab at each flower centre, is one of the most popular singles. Seen here in the company of yellow loosestrife (*Lysimachia punctata*), the mock orange flowers in early summer.**

Honeysuckle is a natural inhabitant of wood and woodland edge, widely distributed as native and naturalized plants all over the northern hemisphere. The English would say that the woodbine *Lonicera periclymenum* has the best scent, but whether the trumpets are pollinated by hummingbirds or bumble bees, they are welcome in gardens (with the exception of *Lonicera japonica*, an Asian species which, though it behaves perfectly well in Europe, has become a serious weed in North America). Honeysuckle is at its best climbing up through a hedge or trellised wall, or over an old tree stump, although it is advisable not to encourage it up young trees as the winding stem can hold back growth. The scent is incomparable and an important constituent of a summer evening.

Clematis montana is a vigorous climber that, unlike most clematis, enjoys a woodland situation and will happily romp up trees and over hedges or stumps, producing masses of small, slightly scented flowers. The cultivars *C. m.* var. *wilsonii* and 'Odorata', both white-flowered kinds, are particularly strongly scented, bringing a delicious sweet vanilla to the early summer woodland garden. These clematis do not require pruning and are hardy and usually trouble-free.

In recent years, an increasing number of named cultivars of *Clematis montana* has become generally available. Some are steady older varieties, such as the pink *C. m.* var *rubens* from the 1950s and 'Tetrarose' from the 1960s; others are newly bred, such as 'Warwickshire Rose' and 'Mayleen', which have satin-pink flowers against bronze foliage and are strongly vanilla-scented. The pink forms need to be used with care so as not to look artificial in the woodland garden. They look well alongside paths and are a very handsome and splendid covering for large boundary walls, growing high into a tree or bringing a light touch to a large heavy conifer. *Clematis montana* is reliably hardy over most of Europe and North America, but is not yet as well known as it deserves to be.

There is a vast number of ivy cultivars, some of them extremely fussy and artificial-looking and therefore best kept well away from the woodland-edge garden, where the accent is on a natural effect.

Choose instead one of the glossy, dark green ivies that are closer to the species, such as *Hedera helix* subsp. *hibernica* or perhaps *H. h.* 'Deltoidea'. There are also many quite natural small-leaved sports of the common ivy that look well in a small garden. Some such as 'Glacier' are attractively variegated and can lighten a dark corner. 'Green Ripple', as the name implies, has a leaf that looks as if it were underwater. Ivies naturally grow up trees, and they will also cover bare ground, rooting from their stems.

The white lacecap hydrangea, now known as *Hydrangea anomala* subsp. *petiolaris*, is not uncommon in gardens, although it is not often grown up trees. It can look very attractive in this situation, because you have a clear view of the flowers and, in winter, of the handsome, flaking, cinnamon-coloured bark of the trunk and twigs. It is self-clinging, but appreciates a certain amount of support in the early months while it is getting established.

The golden hop (*Humulus lupulus* 'Aureus') is a vigorous and attractive plant that is eye-catching without appearing too garish when seen growing into a tree or large shrub. The ornamental vine (*Vitis coignetiae*), usually grown over walls, can also be grown up the trunk of a large tree, making a dramatic swirl of foliage and giving an autumn colour of fiery crimson and scarlet.

Roses such as *Rosa* 'Complicata', or one of the rambling varieties that are able to tolerate a degree of dryness and shade, also make a lovely show growing up into a tree in a woodland-edge situation.

BELOW **A beautifully toned combination of shrubs and climbers: white *Clematis* 'Silver Moon' growing through blue-leaved *Rosa glauca*, with fluffy-flowered meadow rue (*Thalictrum aquilegifolium*) and *Clematis* 'Niobe' peeping through to the right.**

OPPOSITE **Summer-flowering honeysuckle (*Lonicera periclymenum*) is among the most beautiful and sweetest-smelling of plants. Honeysuckle is traditionally planted around doorways so that the scent can be enjoyed to the full; it is at its best on walls and fences or over dead trees.**

TREES

A mature tree is a tremendous gift to a garden. Whatever else you plant will certainly fall short of the grandeur of a tree that has grown through several generations of human activity. Gardeners all over the world know this and will not have anything to do with the belief of the ignorant that a tree 'takes all the goodness out of the soil'. Ryan Gainey, the American garden designer, moving to his garden in Decatur near Atlanta, Georgia, noted first 'a beautiful white oak, a winged elm of good size, and a male American holly as my gardening companions'. Beth Chatto, who set up a garden in the notoriously dry county of Essex, argues forcibly that you should take out redundant plants that are well past their best but have the sense to recognize 'a rare antique' – in her case six old oaks that had formed part of a farm boundary. Both these gardeners rose to the task and within a few years had glorious and individual gardens flourishing beneath their fine old trees.

A large tree or group of mature trees presents an obvious starting place for a woodland-edge garden, using the shapes of the trees and the fall of the shade to guide the stages of the design. Having rid the ground of weeds, you need to dig, aerate and mulch the compacted soil where you can, planting where possible in the most fertile patches. Cyclamen in particular appreciate a good mulching after planting. Old orchard areas, or ancient fruit-tree groupings situated at the end of the garden, also make a good basis for a woodland-edge plot.

BELOW **This beautiful, white, double-flowered flowering cherry has an unusually open and generous branching habit. The owners are still puzzling its precise identification but are delighted with its annual showing in early spring.**

If you are starting a new garden and have no trees, consider carefully which species to plant. As most modern gardens are on a smaller scale than those of the past, it is a shame to plant a tree that is inherently too large so that you have to lop it or, even worse, take it out because it threatens roofs, windows and drains. Do not forget that trees can also cause a nuisance by being too tall; Leyland and Lawson cypresses, planted as boundary trees in small gardens, continue to cause misery to light-starved owners and neighbours. There are plenty of beautiful, small and medium-sized trees that bring unalloyed pleasure.

For a natural style of gardening, choose trees that are close to those native to the landscape or non-natives that will fit in comfortably. Trees are larger and make their presence felt more emphatically than ground-hugging plants, so avoid trees with violent or unnatural colouring of flowers or foliage. Trees such as oak and beech cast deep shade, while others, such as ash and birch, allow more light through to the ground below. You could choose trees for elegance of shape, for rapid (or slow) growth or to provide ornamental or edible fruit.

LEFT Paper birch (*Betula papyrifera*) is a North American species with pale bark that peels in thin layers. A tall tree, its leaves turn through yellow to golden orange in autumn. Grown individually or in small groups, as here, it is seen to perfection in open ground.

A GUIDE TO SELECTING TREES FOR YOUR GARDEN

SMALL TREES

Chinese witch hazel/Ozark witch hazel
Hamamelis mollis/Hamamelis vernalis
over 3m (10ft) • rich foliage, good autumn colour • neutral to acid soil • sun–very light shade • many varieties of both species • flowers sweet scented in *H. mollis*, pleasantly pungent in *H. vernalis*

Hazel *Corylus avellana*
many species and named varieties over 3m (10ft) • ornamental with edible nuts • coppices well • any soil • sun–medium shade • other attractive species include the American hazel (*C. americana*) and *C. cornuta*

Whitebeam *Sorbus aria*
Rowan *Sorbus aucuparia*
and other species and varieties 9–15m (30–49ft) • lovely foliage, pretty flowers and fruits • easily grown in most well-drained fertile soils • sun–light shade • *S. aria* tolerant of alkaline soil; *S. aucuparia* plant in any soil but is tolerant of extreme acidity

MEDIUM-SIZED TREES

Holly *Ilex aquifolia*
15m (49ft) • many other species and varieties • including dwarf ones • most soils; US species prefer neutral or acidic soil • most conditions • US x *aquipernyi* hybrids hardier than Eurasian types • adaptable evergreen tree will withstand pollution and windy seaside situations

Birch *Betula utilis* var. *jacquemontii*
River Birch *Betula nigra*
15m (49ft) *jacquemontii* has pure white bark • *B. nigra* has shaggy pink-brown bark • most soils • in USA grow well by rivers; where summers are less hot will grow in sunlight or shady edge of wood • lightish conditions • airy, open trees, very good in new open gardens; give light shade • bulbs do well beneath

Green ash *Fraxinus pennsylvanica*
Ash *Fraxinus excelsior* 'Jaspidea'
20–23m (66–70ft) 'Jaspidea' is a golden-green form of the common ash • any soil type • sun–mid-shade • in many places in Europe, common ash (*F. excelsior*) will self-seed readily – may be coppiced

LARGER TREES

English oak *Quercus robur*
Red Oak *Quercus rubra*
26–32m (85–105ft), fine spreading trees • *Q. rubra* has pointed leaf lobes and good autumn colour • most soils; *Q. robur* often better on heavy clays; *Q. rubra* good for cooler areas • most places • long-lived, beautiful trees

Scots pine *Pinus sylvestris*
Bishop pine *Pinus muricata*
18m (59ft) and over • *P. sylvestris* red-trunk; *P. muricata* good in exposed maritime areas • most soils except extreme chalk; *P. muricata* good in poor soils • most places • *P. muricata* good in windy conditions • seed from very cold places may produce trees with increased cold resistance

Balsam poplar *Populus trichocarpa*
Populus 'Balsam Spire'
30m (98ft) • rapid-growing sweet-scented • all soil types, including wet • sun to mid-shade • will pollard or take spring pruning; good for screens • will grow readily from cuttings

WATER AND WETLAND

All plants need moisture but some are adapted to thrive in damp ground, while a few can survive in waterlogged bog conditions. The specialized aquatic plants spend their entire life cycles submerged or semi-submerged, some rooted into a bank or the bottom of a pond, others free-floating. If you can discover or contrive a damp area or a pool in your garden, you open the way to a range of plants that is not only endlessly fascinating in itself but also to a habitat that invites a selection of fauna and flora of incredible intricacy and beauty.

Siting a damp garden or pool that will look natural in your garden entails exploring a range of possibilities. The means for making water features in gardens are nowadays so sophisticated that you could make a pool, lake or fountain just about anywhere, suitable or not. It is important not to be hasty but to make considered preparations so that, when you finally achieve your aim and start planting in or beside the water, it will look absolutely natural from the start. Even if you have to make a an artificial construction, try to interfere as little as possible with natural cycles, aiming to integrate your water centrepiece in a way that is as nearly self-sustaining as it can possibly be.

A pond or pool does not have to be situated near a water supply. Once the pond is filled by means of a hose, rainwater will make up for the evaporated water loss, except in very hot weather when it will need topping up. If you create a water spout or rill effect, you will need to run an electricity cable to the pool to provide power for the pump, but the water is continuously recycled. As the world becomes more conscious of the importance of water conservation, schemes for using rainwater run-off (collected in tanks or diverted from drainpipes) to fill and top up garden ponds are becoming increasingly common. This has the extra benefit of providing water that is free both from excess nutrients and cleansing agents.

There are many different ways of introducing water into even a small garden: fountains, rills, steps, simple canals or a simulated area of boggy land. A garden pool with a grassy edge, surrounded by plants, is one of the easiest to accommodate in a garden that has a natural look, where more formal water pieces might look out of place. Once you have the pool to your satisfaction, it is likely that you will want to try something else, such as a rill, spout or pebble pool – water is addictive. The pleasure of the reflected plants, dragonflies, and other creatures that frequent the pool, and the air of tranquil invitation that a pool brings to a garden, make the initial labours seem a very small price compared to the deep and lasting pleasures. The effects of the sound of water should not be underestimated: the trickle of a little rill or the splash of a spout will blend into a natural setting, a counterpoint to bird song and the sounds of bees and other insects.

BELOW **A damp spot, populated by ferns, lady's mantle (*Alchemilla mollis*) and skunk cabbage (*Lysichiton americanum*); deep pink candelabra primroses (*Primula beesiana*) create a springtime element of drama beside the fresh green foliage.**

OPPOSITE **A luxuriant spring scene with yellow flag (*Iris pseudacorus*) and bistort (*Persicaria bistorta* 'Superba') flowering in the damp foreground, while gunnera (*Gunnera manicata*), skunk cabbage (*Lysichiton americanum*) and shrubs typical of marshy ground inhabit the edges and slightly higher ground.**

WETLAND FOR THE ORDINARY GARDEN

Many gardens have a damp section, perhaps indicated by reeds, rushes or creeping buttercup. It is usually the part over which landscape gardeners will shake their heads and suggest expensive systems of drainage that will ruin you and disrupt your existing garden. Surely it is better to take a cue from nature and look for plants that actually enjoy the damp and then take advantage of this extra element in the garden. Damp-loving plants offer tremendous choice. Some, such as irises and water lilies, like sun, while others, such as hostas and *Lysimachia* species (creeping Jenny and yellow loosestrife), prefer shady conditions. This group of plants will take you through the growing season, from the early spring flush of marsh marigolds (*Caltha palustris*) to the damp-loving Michelmas daisies of autumn.

In the past people understood how to use land just as it was. Among the nicest farm habitats were water meadows – low-lying land that flooded in winter and grew a vast range of meadow flowers in spring and summer. A damper area of lawn will support creeping Jenny (*Lysimachia nummularia*), a trailing plant with bright yellow flowers. The lady's smock (*Cardamine pratensis*) has silvery-pink flowers in spring, while the deeper red flowers of ragged robin (*Lychnis flos-cuculi*) and the dark pink spires of purple loosestrife (*Lythrum salicaria*) follow in summer on plants a little higher than the surrounding grasses. American gardeners need to avoid this European native, which has become an extremely aggressive weed in northern parts of the USA, and plant instead the native swamp loosestrife (*Decodon verticillatus*).

ABOVE **A sure sign of damp ground and a reliable performer for such areas, bistort (*Persicaria bistorta*) will naturalize freely. The native species is pale pink, subspecies *P. b. carnea* is a deeper pink, while 'Superba' has more rounded, pale pink flowerheads.**

LEFT **A tranquil damp meadow in a grass ravine with a falling stream and red and white snake's-head fritillary (*Fritillaria meleagris*). The small curved bulbs of this fritillary are more likely to grow well if they are planted in summer before they dry out.**

Meadowsweet (*Filipendula ulmaria*) flies its tall, creamy plumes in late summer and, topping that, queen of the prairies (*F. rubra*) produces a stunning clump of pink flowers on tall stems.

The snake's-head fritillary (*Fritillaria meleagris*) is naturally a plant of meadows that flood in the winter months; it naturalizes well in gardens, including those that are only slightly damp. The good-natured lady's mantle (*Alchemilla mollis*) will also naturalize in grass, where it makes a good foil to astilbe. The latter is native to moist places in mountain ravines, wood margins, and alongside streams in North America and southeastern Asia. The species *Astilbe chinensis* grows to 60cm (2ft), bearing panicles of pink-white flowers in late summer, but you are more likely to come across some of its many hybrids. *A. chinensis* var. *pumila* is small – to 25cm (10in) – with deep pink flowers, while *A. simplicifolia* 'Sprite' is taller – 50cm (20in) – making a dense clump of narrow-leaved foliage with feathery, pale pink flowers in summer. In reliably damp conditions astilbes may be grown in sun or light shade, but in ground that may dry out in summer they prefer partial shade.

Sun-loving day lilies (*Hemerocallis*) like a moist soil that is not waterlogged. In their oriental homelands, they grow in damp meadows and marshy river valleys. Having escaped from gardens, they have become widely naturalized and are often used in wild gardens, where they look best planted in drifts or groups. *Hemerocallis fulva* has big, orange-bronze flowers, while *H. lilioasphodelus* is a semi-evergreen with large, scented, lemon-yellow flowers. Both clump up to a sturdy 1m (3ft) in height and diameter, although there is plenty of choice among the smaller and differently coloured hybrids.

Crocosmia is usually found in flower borders, but it has naturalized itself and will thrive wherever it finds moist, humus-rich soils. I remember the brilliant red *Crocosmia masoniorum* from a clump that was almost the only plant surviving in a ruined garden, its bright flowers indicating where flowerbeds had once been. The hybrid montbretia *Crocosmia* × *crocosmiiflora* (from *C. aurea* × *C. pottsii*), with its smaller orange and red flowers, also naturalizes readily, even though it is a horticultural cultivar, first raised in France in 1880.

ABOVE **Astilbes (*Astilbe*), with their graceful, feathery flowerheads, growing in front of the handsome complementary partners of male fern (*Dryopteris filix-mas*) and royal fern (*Osmunda regalis*). Smaller hybrid astilbes are now available, so they can be grown in even a small marshy or pondside area.**

WETLAND TREES AND SHRUBS

Trees that are suited to damp places include willows (*Salix*), poplars (*Populus*), the glorious liquidamber (*Liquidamber styraciflua*), noted for its autumnal colour, and swamp cypress (*Taxodium distichum*), a particularly beautiful conifer that is unusual in being deciduous. The balsam-scented poplars have glossy, heart-shaped leaves and exude the most delicious resin-like scent through spring and early summer. Black cottonwood (*Populus trichocarpa*) is the species most often found in Europe. These poplars come very easily from cuttings and make a fair-sized, scented tree in a few years, doing well in poor soils. The large, fast-growing *P. balsamifera* – up to 30m (100ft) – is often cited in books but rarely planted. The hybrid 'Balm of Gilead' (*P. x jackii* 'Gileadensis') or 'Ontario Poplar', is medium sized, with strongly scented leaves that are grey-downy beneath.

Alders (*Alnus*), elders (*Sambucus*) and many of the *Sorbus* species, including the mountain ash (*S. aucuparia*), will do well in damp ground. There is also a huge range of willows. White willow (*Salix alba*) and silver willow (*S. alba* f. *argentea*) are large and elegant trees, while the golden-barked corkscrew willow (*S. 'Erythroslexuosa'*) and violet willow (*Salix daphnoides*) are smaller and highly ornamental. Willows and dogwoods with coloured barks, such as the golden-stemmed *S. vitellina* 'Britzensis' and the rich red *Cornus alba* 'Elegantissima', can be cut back annually to keep their growth in check and to produce multiple stems. However, planting willows or poplars will change the immediate environment and begin to dry it out.

Many attractive shrubs also enjoy damp conditions. *Physocarpus opulifolius* 'Luteus' likes an open area, where its yellow foliage shows to its best. Hydrangeas of many kinds thrive in shady damp places. Among some of the larger bushy herbaceous perennials, the popular and sturdy yellow-flowered paeony (*Paeonia mlokosewitschii*) and Chinese rhubarb (*Rheum palmatum*) make very handsome damp-ground plants.

DIPS AND DITCHES

Having a natural stream in your garden must be the greatest joy and I unashamedly envy people who possess this feature. The nearest I have ever come to having one was a shady drainage ditch attached to the end of a small, dry chalky garden, where in winter months and sometimes during the summer a small stream would run. Initially, it had little or no vegetation, but planted with woodland plants it became extremely pretty.

I have seen larger damp ditches, improved by the addition of leaf mould, transformed into a home for primroses, primulas, ferns, hellebores, woodland euphorbias, dicentras and gentians. One side of the ditch will typically get more sun while the other can be a home to shade-loving plants. Damp shade has its own repertoire and creates a wonderful feeling of tropical exuberance in a dip or valley bottom.

Many handsome and compact plants grow well in damp dips and ditches. *Saxifraga fortunei* has delightful foliage and a mass of tiny starry flowers. *Tiarella cordifolia* also has starry flowers, held up in upright racemes. The North American coral flowers (*Heuchera*) produce their tiny blooms in pinks, yellows and reds. All of these plants have foliage of particular beauty, so that they look just as attractive out of flower. Hostas come in large and small sizes with a variety of leaf textures and patterns. These plants are grown principally for their foliage, but they also have

BELOW **This quiet rill under a retaining wall creates humidity for mosses, ferns and marginal plants. Hardy geraniums and wild strawberries (*Fragaria vesca*) have been chosen to cascade on the bank, while an informal repetition of *Iris sibirica* and *Zantedeschia*, backed by mulleins, lines the opposite side.**

algae from reproducing, since they require sunlight in order to grow. An easier method, particularly for smaller ponds and pools, is to allow surface-floating plants such as duckweeds or fairy moss (*Azolla filiculoides*) to almost cover the pond. They satisfactorily exclude light until other aquatic plants can take over. It is then an easy matter to skim off the excess duckweed or fairy moss. Water snails also help establish a balance in a pond or pool by grazing the algae. Avoid using proprietary chemical remedies or conditioners, since these not only usually generate new problems but create a chemical dependency.

RIGHT Pickerel weed (*Pontederia cordata*) is a vigorous **aquatic and marginal plant. The tawny-orange day lilies behind like damp soil and plenty of hot sun in order to flower as profusely as this, while the yellow *Lysimachia* behind prefers to grow in a little shade.**

Bulrush/greater reedmace
Typha latifolia
Pond and pool edges; dark
brown flowerheads; sun or
shade; vigorous growth.

Yellow flag
Iris pseudacorus
Moist soil or shallow
water; yellow flowers in
late spring.

Fringed water lily
Nymphoides peltata
Clear yellow-fringed
flowers above small, heart-
shaped leaves in summer.

Water soldier
Stratiotes aloides
Aquatic floating perennial;
leafy rosette of narrow
leaves that sinks to the
bottom in autumn.

Bogbean
Menyanthes trifoliata
Marginal; pretty, three-
lobed leaves; fringed,
pale pink flowers.

Pickerel weed
Pontaderia cordata
Glossy, lance-shaped
leaves; rich blue flower-
spikes bloom in
summer and autumn.

Hornwort *Ceratophyllum*
demersum Submerged
aquatic oxygenator; finely-
forked leaves; sinks to the
bottom in winter.

A NATURAL STYLE POND

It is important when siting a garden pond to make the right preparations so that, by the time you start planting in or beside the water, it will look absolutely natural. Remember also that a pond does not have to be situated near a water supply. Once it is full, rainwater will make up for most of the evaporated water loss, except in very hot weather or a drought.

Once you have decided on the right place for the pond, start by laying out the shape with pegs and hosepiping. Keep in mind that ponds that have at least one deeper part (about 1m (3ft)) tend to be easier to manage and are better at self-regulation. It is conventional to create a shallower outer shelf, stepping down to a deeper part – if you intend to keep your plants in perforated pots this gives them something to stand on. In many ways a gently sloping saucer shape is preferable for a more natural style of pond as this allows you to add a layer of gravel and soil to plant into.

When you are satisfied with the shape and dimensions, you can begin to dig out the hole. If you intend to have a pump, install a channel to the edge of the pond for the cable (and protective plastic conduit). It pays to be as neat as possible and to remember that you will need to go down about 15cm (6in) deeper than you intend to allow for the space taken up by insulation and liner. Cut a 15cm (6in) lip all the way around the perimeter of the pond to lay the overlap liner on. If you want a small swampy area next to the pond, extend this lip to make a bowl shape that can be refilled in with soil later. The best linings are made from butyl or EPDM (ethylene-propylene diene monomer) as these are tough enough to last about fifty years. Your supplier will be able to help you calculate the amount of waterproof liner you will require, but a simple rule of thumb for liner width and length is to measure the maximum width plus twice the depth of the pond, by the maximum length plus twice its depth.

Before you put your liner in place, pick out any sharp objects. If your garden is clay, or clay and flint, it is well worth cushioning the liner with a proprietary underlay. For best effect, another layer should go on top of the liner, to protect it from direct sunlight and also to provide a non-slippery base for your soil layer. Position the liner carefully so that it fits smoothly and without stretch, moulding the form of the pond (and bog area if you have one); then fit the overlay and gently add the layer of soil and gravel. Do not run a hosepipe directly into the pond or you will create a cloud of mud, but place it on a piece of underlay so that it trickles in gently and slowly, gradually amplifying until the pond is full. Use the topsoil elsewhere in the garden and dispose of the dank subsoil. The gravel layer is optional, but it helps keep the soil layer in place, and also acts as extra protection for the liner which, if left uncovered, can deteriorate in sunlight.

HOW TO MAKE A POND

1 Dig out the pond, keeping just inside the designated boundary. Don't forget to loosen turfs about 15cm (6in) outside the pegged area under which you will need to secure the liner overlap.

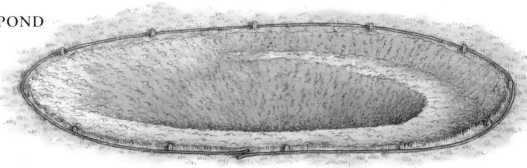

2 Check the sides are level with a plank and spirit level. Take out the pegs, remove the turfs, and then lay the sand, underlay and liner, before replacing the turfs. Continue to make adjustments to the sides by taking out subsoil and replacing the turf until the levels are correct all round.

3 Carefully add the soil and gravel layers, patting it into shape. Take care not to puncture the liner. Fill slowly by allowing the hose to trickle the water in over a piece of underlay or flat stone. Allow the full pond to settle for a day or two before gently introducing plants.

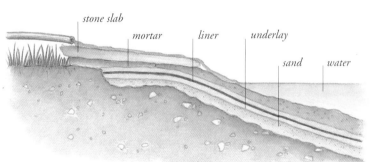

stone slab

mortar   *liner*   *underlay*

sand   *water*

ABOVE **A soft mixture of plants around a pond with the early-flowering *Prunus*, known as 'Tai Haku', the great white cherry, situated so that its foliage reflects with the sky in the water. Nearby on the bank is the handsome royal fern (*Osmunda regalis*) with shrubs and grasses.**

4 You can plant directly into the layer of soil and gravel, causing as little disturbance as possible. The water will cloud but soon clear. Check with the nursery that you are getting the correct depth of planting, and match plant vigour to the size of your pool. Introduce floating oxygenating plants.

WATER AND WETLAND

It was astonishing to find pond skaters trying out the surface of the newly made, little semi-circular pool in our garden almost before the water filling it had stopped running. This dash to take advantage of an additional habitat is not an isolated occurrence. There seems to be a bush telegraph that lets local wildlife know at once where a pond is being established. Initially there may be disproportionate plant growth in one area or another, although in most cases the pool will settle into a balance that requires little or no interference.

It is a good idea to establish some oxygenating aquatic plants in a new pool, to provide for the water snails and microfauna and prevent the water from becoming stale and stagnant. A friend who has a thriving pond will probably be only too pleased to give you a handful of these plants, and you are likely to inherit a few water snails along with them. Pondweeds, such as the Canadian pondweed (*Elodea canadensis* and the denser, more greyish-green *E. callitrichoides*), the hornworts (*Ceratophyllum demersum* and *C. submersum*), as well as the beautiful

feathery *Myriophyllum aquaticum*, are all easily grown and look attractive. Although they will grow readily from pieces thrown into the pond, it is better to tuck them into the silt that lies at the bottom of the pond. Floating fairy weed (*Azolla caroliniana*) is a pretty floating species which, like the water hyacinth (*Eichhornia crassipes*), can be simply dropped into the water.

Which aquatic plants you choose is a matter of personal preference and local climatic conditions. However, the experience of the last few decades in several parts of the world has shown the importance of disposing of any surplus onto the compost heap and not into a nearby waterway. Alien water plants have caused serious problems through rapid and vigorous colonization. Water hyacinth, for example, has become so pernicious that it has been banned in some American states, although it remains an attractive and useful pond plant in a garden environment.

Underwater plants also provide cover for secretive underwater creatures. Water snails (species of *Lymnaea*, *Planorbis* and *Viviparus*) are more

BELOW **A simple but striking raised brick pool and birdbath are the main features of this small scent- and colour-filled terrace, with its billows of lady's mantle (*Alchemilla mollis*) and easy-going *Lilium regale* in large pots. Cut lady's mantle back after flowering and it will soon make fresh growth.**

acceptable than their terrestrial counterparts, because they clean up decaying animal matter and are generally much less concerned with nibbling living plants. Water spiders, water beetles, pond skaters and water boatmen are among the other larger invertebrates that find their way into garden ponds, along with the larvae and nymph forms of dragonflies, stoneflies and mayflies.

Frogs, toads and newts also take full advantage of garden ponds even if they do not breed in it, the species varying according to country. It does not take long for the common frog (*Rana temporaria*) to visit new ponds in most parts of northern Europe, while further south the little tree frog *Hyla meridionalis* is a frequent visitor. In the USA, green frogs (*R. clamitans*) and bullfrogs (*R. catesbiana*) are the most usual garden frogs, with some *Hyla* species being found in warmer states. Moving frogspawn to a new pond used to be recommended, but red-leg virus has spread so malignantly in Europe, this practice is now best avoided.

If the pond has inviting shallows, birds certainly will visit to drink and wash, and in times of drought thirsty mammals may be drawn to the water.

ABOVE **A natural beach effect: this shaded, humid, stone-edged pool, contains small water lilies (***Nymphaea***)and water hawthorn (***Aponogeton distachyos***), overhung with clumps of bergenia on one side and giving onto rocks and pebbles on the other.**

LEFT **The simplest ideas are often the best: stone steps set into a bank, with a carefully controlled water flow and a natural woodland edging of snowdrops, violets and wild arum, makes a fall of great charm and naturalness.**

HOT SPOTS AND DRY PLACES

All green plants need sun and water to live, but in different proportions. Specialist adaptations enable plant life to survive in substantially different climatic conditions. This section of the book looks at the vast range of plants growing readily in hot, dry parts of the temperate areas of the world and suggests ways of using and combining them in gardens for a natural effect that is also in tune with the local landscape.

Even in countries where rain falls plentifully, drought is becoming a common experience. Garden use as a proportion of total consumption is very small, but it is focused precisely on those times when resources can least cope with extra requirement. It makes sense, therefore, to look at the water economy of a garden in terms of self-sufficiency, while at the same time exploring the gardening opportunities presented by drought-resistant plants.

Hot-country and drought-tolerant plants have developed different ways of dealing with their situation and climate. In the Mediterranean, for example, they have a double dormancy, closing down their growing systems in the hottest part of the year to protect themselves from dangerously high water evaporation. Some plants, including many of the culinary herbs, develop the capacity to synthesize oils that decrease evaporation and defend the plant from insect damage. Leaves are inrolled to minimize the number of water-transpiring stomata exposed to the sun. Foliage may be dark, leathery and protective or reflectively pale in greys and silvers, with downy or curved surfaces and stems that may be angled away from the sun's glare. It takes only a little investigation to uncover a wide choice for a garden in what at first may seem to be a dry, barren and infertile plot.

Such conditions are precisely those in which some of the slow-growing, drought-tolerant plants thrive best. Lavenders and many of the herbs do rather poorly in fertile, moist conditions, where they grow too fast and the easy conditions fail to trigger the processes that make their valued, complex aromatic oils. Silvery-leaved shrubby plants make a worthy contribution to a dry garden in the form of artemisias (*Artemisia absinthium* or the smaller *A. pontica*, with its daintily cut, woolly foliage), the bushy dorycniums (*Dorycnium penataphyllum* or softly downy *D. hirsutum*) and the indispensable cotton lavender (*Santolina chamaecyparissus*). There are softly, silvery perennials, such as the tall bushy *Perovskia atriplicifolia*, with its strong, violet-blue, late-season flowers, the furry *Stachys byzantina* that makes such a good foil to bright plants such as sun-loving geraniums, rose verbena (*Verbena canadensis*), or the many kinds of bulbs, such as the summer wild onion (*Allium cernuum*), that rise rapidly to flower in dry conditions and then lie low beneath the baking ground. The key to a naturalistic display of such plants, whether in a large or small area, is to build up a flow of plants that associate well, trying to avoid overcrowded, very busy designs. This is a kind of garden where you bask in heat, colour and scent.

BELOW **Autumn joy (*Sedum* 'Herbstfreude') loves hot places and stays handsome throughout the season, with its grey-green spring foliage, its colourful, flat summer flowerheads and its autumn contrasts; in winter the seeds are welcomed by birds and insects.**

OPPOSITE **A dry, rocky garden superbly set among the Californian hills. In contrast to the tall umbrella pine (*Pinus pinea*), the rocky plateau has a lowish informal planting of herbs, such as rosemary, lavender, mound-forming dry-ground shrubs and ground-hugging species.**

NATURAL DESIGNS FOR HOT, DRY PLACES

BELOW **A concert of hot midsummer colour, with pink-headed *Allium aflatunense*, lemon-yellow *Sisyrinchium striatum* and hardy geraniums as the main players. The old-fashioned chimney pot provides an informal sculptural effect.**

In reality most gardeners use far more water than is necessary or even desirable. Only seedlings and newly-planted specimens really need extra watering, and even this should be limited. Choose the right kinds of plant for a dry situation and conserve rain when it does fall, while keeping the soil in good heart with compost and mulches, and the garden can look beautiful while requiring a minimum of extra water, or perhaps none at all. The beautiful bulbs, perennials and shrubs that enjoy hot, dry conditions are tempting to any gardener, although it is not always easy to design a place for them within the garden as a whole. They tend to struggle and call for special care if planted in normally moist and fertile beds in competition with more robust plants. This group of plants prefers conditions more akin to those of their origins, although it sometimes takes a little ingenuity to place them appropriately. Sometimes the answer is obvious: a bed with full sun for most of the day, for example. Most gardens,

however, can provide suitable conditions if you seek them: the base of a south-facing wall or the paved surface of a terrace or patio; the upper part of a bank or the cracks and interstices in a wall; a small bank of well-drained ground, perhaps a place where a previous householder has dumped hardcore or more general building rubble, with shallow, fast-draining soil that quickly becomes warm in the summer time.

The actual design will be influenced by the shape of the hot, dry area and its boundary walls or paths, but as a general rule, the planting can be fairly sparse. While you need to make sure that all the plants are seen to their best advantage, it is not necessary – indeed it looks rather forced – if you create a tiered hierarchy as in a conventional border. In their native condition, most of the plants of hot, dry lands are scattered over the terrain, tall ones such as asphodel (*Asphodelus albus*) or verbascums rising high, sprawlers such as mat-forming thymes (*Thymus serpyllum*) and candytuft (*Iberis sempervirens*) carpeting the ground in between, and medium-sized alliums and gauras dotted amongst them. Silvery- and blue-grey-leaved shrubs, such as lavender or perovskia, provide substance within the design.

PLANTING PLAN FOR HOT, DRY PLACES

A hot, dry site should be planted to glimmer in a haze of heat, colour and scent. Including a selection of native plants seems to anchor the design; other plants can be added to build up sequence, colour and texture. It is important that the ground is well drained (adding grit if necessary), since many of the plants typical of this habitat will perish if they become waterlogged.

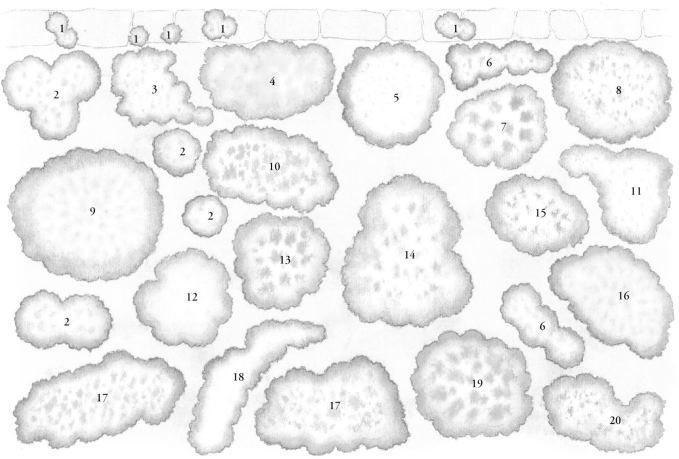

KEY TO PLANTING

1 Rosy garlic *Allium roseum*
2 *Verbascum blattaria* 'Albiflorum'
3 *Allium cristophii*
4 *Euphorbia characias wulfenii*
5 *Verbascum chaixii* 'Album'
6 Vervain *Valeriana officinalis*
7 *Agapanthus campanulatus*

8 *Ceanothus* 'Cynthia Postan'
9 Grass *Stipa calamagrostis*
10 Pink *Dianthus carthusianorum*
11 Perennial flax *Linum perenne*
12 Oriental poppy *Papaver orientale* 'Cedric Morris'
13 Opium poppy *Papaver somniferum*
14 Lavender *Lavandula angustifolia*

15 *Perovskia atriplicifolia*
16 Giant feather grass *Stipa gigantea*
17 *Geranium sanguineum*
18 *Gaura lindheimeri*
19 *Kniphofia* 'Prince Igor'
20 Thyme *Thymus vulgaris*

GARDEN WALLS

It is not as well appreciated as it should be that the flora of cliff faces in mountainous regions finds a happy counterpart in stone and brick walls in the garden. Such walls, often self-seeded, can have a stunning impact. I recall a high limestone wall aflame with fragrant wallflowers (*Erysimum cheiri*) in reds, oranges and golds. Although in itself quite uninteresting, a town garden wall near where I live is smothered in rock plants. There are *Aubrieta*, yellow corydalis (*Corydalis lutea*) and ivy-leaved toadflax

(*Cymbalaria muralis*) spilling out in bright patches, as well as small cotoneasters and buddlejas; plants that are common and unexceptional in themselves but superb growing brilliantly against the grey wall in the full sun. Recently *Erigeron karvinskianus* from Central America has joined the scheme. The tiny daisy flowers of this plant (sometimes known as Mexican fleabane) open off-white and fade through pink to crimson. It has become a favourite in gardens, whence it has truanted and become widely naturalized all over Europe.

ABOVE **Mexican fleabane (*Erigeron karvinskianus*) is here thoroughly naturalized and at home in a warm, dry-stone wall. These diminutive, daisy-type plants love to grow in crevices in walls and between paving.**

LEFT A dry-stone wall with common polypody (*Polypodium vulgare*), variegated ivy and catmint (*Nepeta* x *faassenii*) growing in it. The yellow daisies of *Doronicum* x *excelsum* 'Harpur Crewe' and pale blue *Veronica gentianoides* grow in the meadow beyond.

Rock gardens *per se* have a slightly old-fashioned feel, and nowadays there is justifiable environmental concern about selling stone from natural limestone pavements for use as rock-garden material. Such interventionist rockeries would be out of place in a garden designed on natural principles, but in any case they almost always look hopelessly unnatural inside a wider landscape to which they are entirely alien. On purely practical grounds, the vertical rock garden provided by a wall takes up far less space than its sprawling predecessor.

To establish alpines in walls some books give instructions that tell you to scrape out mortar and stuff in small plants or seeded compost but, in my view, colonization is usually more successful when carried out by the plants themselves. This is difficult in a new wall with hard pointing. In such cases, making a few scrapes to create small ledges between the brick and the mortar makes it possible for a little organic matter to accumulate and for air- or bird-borne seeds to germinate. Grow suitable plants in pots or in beds nearby in the hope that seeds will be blown or carried into the wall. If you are building or repairing a wall, use a soft, lime-based mortar which is more inviting to plants than the harder cements. Dry-stone walls are attractive in themselves as well as to plants and can almost be considered a kind of vernacular sculpture in their own right.

ABOVE Grey stone steps and paving beautifully set off by sweeps of pink-red and purple *Salvia officinalis* 'Purpurascens' and red valerian (*Centranthus ruber*). When the flowers die back, the salvia foliage and the ivy on the steps will create a softening effect in dark- and blue-green.

WALL BORDERS

The base of a wall is much dryer than is usually recognized. This can be a disadvantage and accounts for the failure to thrive, or even the death of, many climbing plants and shrubs that need normal water conditions but have been planted close to the wall. It can, however, provide a strip of brilliance as the base of an almost vertical mini garden. There is a wide range of bulbs, climbing plants and perennials which need dry conditions and will do well in this wall-hugging mini habitat. The narrowest of strip borders alongside a south- or south-east facing wall can support an incredible range of plants, including herbs, climbing roses, wall-trained shrubs, bulbs and annuals. Enrich the dry soil with some compost now and again, and you will be surprised at how readily the plants grow. The heat from the wall itself tends to bring flowers on earlier in spring and to prolong the season after summer has passed.

The wallside strip border can be very varied. Climbing roses, such as 'Handel' and 'Seagull', and *Clematis* 'Jackmanii' and 'Hagley Hybrid' can be interspersed with evergreens such as pyracanthas and ivy, with tulips, narcissi and ornamental onions (*Allium*) at the base to provide seasonal distraction, along with herbs such as mints, marjoram and parsley. Shrub roses, such as 'Félicité Perpétue' 'Pink Perpétue', with drought-tolerant sedums and honesty, grow alongside shrubs that can sustain cutting back, such as butterfly bush (*Buddleja davidii*), forsythia, *Choisya ternata*, flowering quince (*Chaenomeles japonica*) and *Viburnum tinus*. Such a strip requires some attention in the form of pruning, particularly of the climbing plants, which can be brought down by strong winds; however, the multiplicity of plants tends to keep weeds out.

To give wall-border shrubs and climbers a good start, plant them in a large hole, enriched with good soil, compost and a handful of seaweed meal. Position the plants so that shoots or branches form outwards along the length of the wall. Prune out shoots that grow forwards. Climbing plants such as ivies (*Hedera*) and Virginia creeper (*Parthenocissus*) are self-clinging, while others, such as the climbing hydrangea (*Hydrangea anomala* subsp. *petiolaris*), will climb unaided up a tree but like a little help to get going on a wall. Clematis require a trellis or wires stretched along the wall around which they can twine. Roses, Japanese quince (*Chaenomeles*) and other plants with stout shoots, can be tied onto purpose-made nails secured into the wall. Bulbs can be planted quite densely, and it is worth remembering that sweet peas make a pretty and fragrant show on a warm wall

ABOVE **A mixture of plants for hot, dry conditions:** *Geum* 'Red Wings', with spiky, purple-tinged *Eryngium* x *oliverianum* **growing through it and the yolk-coloured flowers of** *Helichrysum* 'Schwefellicht' **in the foreground.**

RIGHT **Tree poppy** (*Romneya coulteri*) **thrives in the dry sheltered conditions beneath a window. Native to California and Mexico, this shrubby perennial spreads by suckers.**

OPPOSITE **A corner of a walled garden, with a dry bed that catches the sun with hardy geraniums 'Johnson's Blue' and** *Geranium clarkei* **'Kashmir White' growing with bearded iris and lady's mantle (***Alchemilla mollis***), as well as hummocks of scented single pinks (***Dianthus***).**

A DESIGN FOR DRY GROUND

A naturally dry yard or a dry sunlit bed within an otherwise green garden can provide the basis for dry habitat plants. A model that comes to mind for such a plot is that of the dry stream bed. Many rivers throughout the world dry out in summer and run only in the rainy season, and the natural flora of such places is often spectacular. In many regions of Britain these habitats are known as winterbournes, while in the southwestern USA they are the familiar arroyos. Unfortunately, there are now many places where a sinking water table has meant that dry beds have become permanent and the flora has changed as the bed, lacking its wash of water, becomes silted with detritus and acquires a thin soil that supports pioneer plants which in their turn give way to scrub.

A naturalistic dry bed takes plants from different stages of this development. It differs from the gravel bed that garden designers frequently recommend as an alternative to grass in its informality and the self-sustaining nature of the planting. Where possible it should be made from locally available natural materials. In some cases this might be gravel, but only if the colour and textures match those of the garden and its local surroundings. In a rocky area I have seen flat, low pieces of rock making a small but captivating horizontal rock garden.

Dry-country plants love growing through flagstone paving and brick yards, and a semi-ruined, secret garden atmosphere can be created by letting plants grow up like this in a selected area. One of the nicest examples I have seen was a small bricked area in a very dry region of England, where an outbuilding had been demolished, leaving only the brick flooring. This had been colonized by hundreds of Pasque flowers, which had found the right amount of heat and dryness, having come originally from a nearby flowerbed where they had not thrived. Against the old red brick these spring-flowering species – generally found on calcareous, close-grazed hillsides – looked perfectly at home, with their purple petals and lovely cobwebbed seedheads.

Pathways that are not in regular mainline use can also harbour a range of plants. Rock roses (*Helianthmum*), – a widespread genus that is found in meadows and scrubland in Europe, Asia, Africa and both North and South America (and has a full complement of brilliantly coloured hybrids) – looks spectacular in summer. It likes nothing better than to root in the crevices between flagstones and turn a pathway into a river of colour at midsummer. To keep them shapely and to ensure you get a good show each year, cut helianthemums back hard after they have flowered to prevent them from sprawling too much, especially when they may block a path.

Perennials such as Mexican fleabane (*Erigeron karvinskianus*), the viola known as heartsease, wild pansy or Johnny jump-up (*Viola tricolor*), thymes and daisies are pretty colonizers. Foxglove (*Digitalis purpurea*), verbascum (*Verbascum blattaria*) and other large biennials can find their way to less used pathways and can be tolerated as long as they are not actually blocking the way. Annuals, too, find their place, in the form of the common poppies (*Papaver rhoeas*), Welsh poppies (*Meconopsis cambrica*) and royal-blue larkspurs (*Consolida ajacis*), while bulbous plants such as three-cornered leek (*Allium triquetum*), Spanish bluebell (*Hyacinthoides hispanica*) and plants of the iris family, such as sisyrinchiums and the dwarf iris (*Iris reticulata*), may invade gravel paths. To harbour a range of plants, the pathway needs crevices, cracks or an open structure.

ABOVE **A setting that is umistakeably hot climate : the bold architecture of cacti (mostly opuntias and barrel-like *Echinocactus*), palms, grasses, agaves and palm-like plantains (*Musa*) dominates this part of a sun-baked, rocky Italian garden.**

LEFT **The flowerheads of the pink-lavender allium (*Allium christophii*) rise above a silvery white carpet of velvet-leaved lamb's ears, (*Stachys byzantina* 'Silver Carpet'). This non-flowering cultivar is used principally as a backdrop for showier flowers.**

IRREGULAR HERB GARDENS

Over the last decade geometry has dominated the style of herb gardens. Squares, circles and more complicated variations are picked out in dwarf box, the herbs arranged in patterns within them. Charming as formal gardens can be, nothing could be further from the way herbs grow in their native places in the shallow, baked soils of the Causses or the garrigue. Our most valued culinary herbs look best and are at their most aromatic dotted over a landscape that looks on the face of it too infertile to support plant life. In the wild these plants move. They utilize the mineral resources on one piece of ground and then grow outwards to explore adjacent land; the piece left bare will later be recolonized by another species with different requirements.

This movement also occurs in herb gardens and is why formal designs are difficult to manage, since the plants prefer not to stay neatly positioned but want to migrate. A more naturalistic plan for a herb garden keeps the soil poor, aiming for slower but more strongly flavoured growth, and allows the plants to progress within their allotted space. There usually has to be some weeding and pruning, since most garden conditions will be wetter and more fertile than the place of origin, but it is an easier form of management and, in its gentler, more relaxed way, an attractive means of growing herbs.

The landscapes of the Mediterranean are large and open, bounded by mountains and low, wooded and rocky outcrops. Similarly, over many other places in the world, herbs grow in grassland on rocky hillsides; you find species of thyme and Pasque flower in China growing in the harsh landscape around the Great Wall, while many herbs valued in the Americas are found in poor gravelly ground or within rocky landscapes. Poor soil in a warm situation can be found in most gardens (but rarely framed in the elemental landscapes). Natural planting dispenses with the conventional formal element, but there still needs to be definition so that the dry herb garden fits within the garden design as a whole.

A sense of overall design can be made by means of paths around the herb area (which also makes the plants easy to reach for culinary purposes). If you live in a region with natural rock, the herb garden can

BELOW **Dark-flowered French lavender** (*Lavandula stoechas*), **with cotton lavender** (*Santolina chamaecyparissus*) **and upright bushes of rosemary** (*Rosmarinus officinalis*), **interspersed with common lavender** (*Lavandula angustifolia*) **and euphorbia in a boulder-strewn, city herb garden.**

flow from a close-mown lawn into a rock-strewn area, with herbs grown in and around the low rocks and boulders. Another approach is to set aside a self-contained part of the garden especially for herbs. In both cases the composition can include physic herbs as well as culinary ones, although it is important to remember that big burly plants, such as angelica, fennel (*Foeniculum vulgare*), lovage (*Levisticum officinale*), elecampane (*Inula helenium*) and cone flower (*Echinacea purpurea*), take up a good deal of space and can shade or overwhelm smaller, low-growing herbs, especially if allowed to self-seed. One plant of these will provide you with height in the herb garden and also with more than enough material for use in the kitchen, whereas you will probably want several kinds of thyme and marjoram and many different pinks (*Dianthus*).

Our herb gardens are, in fact, extremely cosmopolitan. Basil (*Ocimum basilicum*), used all around the world and so strongly associated with the pasta and olive oils of the Mediterranean basin, was imported to the Mediterranean from the Old World tropics before Roman times. Marjoram (*Origanum vulgare*), a European native, has naturalized readily in the northern USA. Many herbs can be transplanted and will naturalize, although it is important to remember not to spoil them by fertilizing the ground where you intend to grow them. Lavender, thyme and marjoram all lose their piquancy in fertile soils.

Research trials have shown that the evening primroses (*Oenothera*) grows well in easier, more fertile conditions than are found in their native home states in the USA, flowering more readily and producing plenty of seed. However, the seeds no longer contain the complex essential fatty acids that are synthesized in more difficult conditions, where this biennial plant often fails in its first winter owing to fungal attack.

Peppermint and parsley are handsome plants which have properties that aid digestion. *Echinacea*, used by native Americans, especially the tribes that live on the Plains, and adopted by early settlers as a remedy for colds, is now used internationally for its anti-viral, anti-fungal and anti-bacterial properties, while because of its capacity to boost the immune system it is also a component in AIDS therapy. The roots and rhizomes are used in modern medicine, harvested after flowering and then washed, chopped and dried. The flower is less potent and therefore not utilized in commercial herbalism, although an infusion makes a useful general tonic.

ABOVE **Informality with herbs: fennel (*Foeniculum vulgare*), chives (*Allium schoenoprasum*) and golden marjoram (*Origanum vulgare* 'Aureum') growing with the cerise and silver *Lychnis coronaria* and oriental poppies.**

LEFT **The big velvety leaves of verbascum contrast with the foliage detail of small plants: the sage *Salvia officinalis* 'Tricolor' and golden marjoram (*Origanum vulgare* 'Aureum'). These are ornamental cultivars.**

DRY BANKS

A dry bank looks superb with statuesque tiers of shrubs, grasses and perennials planted to present a varied composition of foliage that can range from airy and feathery to dense and heavy, and whose colours catch the sun in greens, greys, copper and pewter with the lime and yellow-greens of euphorbias setting up a long-lasting contrast. This kind of planting is practical as well as ornamental, for the plants stabilize the often thin soils of dry banks and help to prevent erosion of steeps banks and terraces.

On a larger bank, drought-resistant trees such as juniper make a dense block of dark, evergreen foliage that can be offset by the larger euphorbias such as *Euphorbia characias characias* (or *E. c. wulfenii*). On an acidic or neutral soil, brooms (*Genista* and *Cytisus*) do well, with a wide range of flower colours ranging from mahogany red-brown to palest creamy-lemon. One of the most attractive and unusual of the broom-like family is *Adenocarpus decorticans*, which originates from Spain and does well on dry soils and

banks, producing brilliant yellow flowers and sensuous, silken, silver leaves. Lavenders (*Lavandula*) and cotton lavenders (*Santolina*) look very attractive on large banks that have a calcareous element. They have the advantage of growing quite slowly and in fairly compact cushions that require relatively little attention. *Santolina pinnata* subsp. *neapolitana*, with its greenish rather than grey foliage and pale yellow flowers, is particularly attractive. Scattered clumps of grasses such as the neat, blue-leaved festucas, the handsome *Helictotrichon sempervirens* and the tall but dainty *Stipa gigantea* provide a necessary contrast to plants with bright flowers, such as magenta angel's fishing rod (*Dierama pulcherrimum*) or bearded irises and mulleins (*Verbascum*).

On very dry, stony and rocky banks sedums, such as *Sedum spectabile* (known as butterfly stonecrop or ice-plant), and saxifrages will readily naturalize, while pinks (*Dianthus*) and small alliums such as *Allium sphaerocephalon* make small bright spots of crimson. Banks should not be planted too thickly nor too diversely in my view. There already exists the drama of the rising ground and the eye should be able to travel from one plant to another enjoying the individual shape, colours and silhouettes. There is nothing to be gained by trying to emulate the crowded bright medley of the conventional border.

OPPOSITE **Plants spill over dry terraces: the wallflower 'Harpur Crewe' flowers below, while *Euphorbia characias characias* makes green-gold candelabras in front of the clipped conifers *Chamaecyparis lawsoniana* 'Fletcheri', sometimes known as 'Mrs Fish's pudding trees'.**

BELOW LEFT **A dry rocky hillside overflows with plants, including *Helleborus argutifolius* in the shade, bamboo in the dappled area and brooms (*Cytisus*), hardy geraniums and silver-leaved shrubs on the sunlit slopes.**

BELOW RIGHT **A naturalized grouping, with dog daisy or ox-eye daisy (*Leucanthemum vulgare*) taking the dominant role, carmine *Lychnis coronaria* as the centrepiece and tiny heartsease violas (*Viola tricolor*) below and poppies (*Papaver rhoeas*) growing in the distance.**

GARDEN MEADOWS

BELOW **After the spring-time orchids, snake's-head fritillaries and daffodils, this summer meadow settles to a simple but beautiful mixture of ox-eye daisies (*Leucanthemum vulgare*) and hawkbit (*Leontodon hispidus*).**

Meadows have a poignant, impressionistic beauty that has touched the hearts and minds of poets and artists from the early Celts to the European and American painters of the nineteenth and early twentieth centuries. It is therefore hardly surprising that we desire to grasp their vision in our gardens. The thrilling medley of grasses and flowers described by the medieval French poet Guillaume de Lorris and his translator, Geoffrey Chaucer, in the *Romaunt of the Rose* still has the power of romance for us in modern times. There is also the idea that, in incorporating a meadow area, we can vary the pace of the garden and escape the grip of the lawnmower and the monotony of close-mown grass.

There are few more attractive ways of improving a grassy area than by making a wildflower meadow. It is generally thought that such meadows require more

space than the conventional lawn but if you choose the species carefully it is possible to have a meadow sward in a tiny area. I have a spring mini meadow consisting simply of snowdrops (*Galanthus nivalis*) and small wild daffodils (*Narcissus pseudonarcissus*), backed up with snake's-head fritillaries (*Fritillaria meleagris*) and, at the shaded edge, dog's-tooth violets (*Erythronium*). Only the daffodils are truly native to my local area, while the others – native to elsewhere in Britain or to southern Europe and the USA – have naturalized in the immediate locality.

Choosing native and naturalized plants on an international basis means that you have an opportunity to design a meadow tailored precisely to your own requirements in terms of flowering time, composition and scale, relating your choice of plant to the wildflowers that grow around you and to the range of plants that grow in similar conditions elsewhere. Most gardens in temperate regions will support a meadow tuned in this way to the local flora and conditions.

The word 'meadow' derives from the old English word *mead*, which is related to the old word for 'mow'. The word 'prairie' has similar origins, deriving from the French *prairie*, which in turn comes from the Latin *pratum*, both meaning 'meadow' and describing habitats dominated by grasses; as does another more recent American designation of prairie, 'pampas', comes from the Quechua word *bamba* meaning 'plain'. The word 'steppe' signifies an extensive grassy plain and has been applied as a proper name to the vast Eurasian grasslands. Although not precise, these different words are used to denote various kinds of grassland, typifying groups of particular kinds of wild flowers. It is possible to mix plants from various geographical meadow types but they may climax at different times and it is therefore preferable to use a distinct kind as a model.

OPPOSITE **Cone flowers (*Echinacea purpurea*) growing in late summer on a bankside, with scented lilies (the vigorous *Lilium speciosum*), lavender-blue agapanthus, coleus (*Solenostemon scutellariodes*) and shrubs. The prominent, orange-brown cones will persist decoratively into the winter if they are not cut.**

HOW TO MAKE A MEADOW

A good way to start making a meadow is to look at the potential of an existing lawn. Even ordinary lawns usually contain several different species of grass, and probably several wildflowers as well. Give your grass its head for a few weeks in spring to see what you have, then augment it with extra plants to build up to a climax of a particular kind. Some examples of suitable plants are given in the guide below (*see also pages 84–93*).

The early spring lawn is the easiest kind of meadow to achieve; planting bulbs in the autumn will produce flowers next spring. It is also the most economical use of space because it can be mown and returned to lawn when bulb foliage has died back. If you can reserve space for another month or so, a spring alpine meadow can follow on from the early bulbs or be designed as a separate entity. It can be mowed back to lawn in summer. In a mild winter, it may be advantageous to mow in early spring, to stop the turf becoming overgrown so that it overwhelms the small meadow flowers. Cease mowing when you see the leaves of these plants beginning to appear. A wildflower lawn, sparkling with small flowers on sturdy, low- to medium-sized plants that can survive regular mowing, is a midsummer option. This looks orderly throughout the year and only involves mowing with the blades set a little higher than usual or allowing patches of lawn flowers a few weeks to grow and flower before mowing again. High-summer wildflower grasslands are lush and romantic but can be returned to roughish lawn after the plants have flowered, so the effect is orderly and neat throughout the winter. A late summer New World prairie has a tall, robust mixture of clumpy grasses and showy flowering plants. The seedheads of grasses such as miscanthus or cone flower (*Echinacea*) can be very attractive and may be left over winter.

WILDFLOWER MEADOWS: A SEASONAL GUIDE

No style of planting more readily evokes the term 'natural garden' than the wildflower meadow. When planted successfully it gives you a mass of flowers and colour for most of the year – from the low-growing spring lawn and alpine meadows, through the wildflower lawns and grasslands of mid- to high summer, to the dramatic high- to late summer flowering of the prairies.

HOW TO MAKE A MEADOW

● Whatever kind of meadow you opt for, the mowings should always be raked off. An old-fashioned wooden rake is the best tool for this job.

● It is easier to establish small plants you have bought or raised separately than to scatter seed that will have to battle with existing grass.

● Do not be seduced into buying bright annuals and arable wildflowers, such as annual poppies, that need the ground to be disturbed and dug over each year – look instead for sturdy perennials.

● Make sure you mow at the right time for your type of meadow – or you will get tussocky grasses making awkward clumps and big plants elbowing out the smaller ones.

SPRING LAWN
Hardy, small, spring-flowering bulbs bloom early in the season through the grass; after mowing the area can be used as normal lawn in small gardens.
SELECTED PLANTS winter aconites (*Eranthis hyemalis*); snowdrops (*Galanthus nivalis*); daffodils (*Narcissus pseudonarcissus*)
MOWING AND CARE After flowering, wait until foliage has died away – mow as normal from late spring. Make sure your winter lawn is well mown and neat. If the snowdrops become congested after a few years, divide them after flowering and replant.

ALPINE MEADOWS
Low-growing plants for spring in temperate regions.
SELECTED PLANTS lady's smock (*Cardamine pratensis*); snake's-head fritillary (*Fritillaria meleagris*); Spanish bluebell (*Hyacinthoides hispanica*); phlox (*Phlox drummondii*); Jacob's ladder (*Polemonium* – European and US species); cowslip (*Primula veris*); primrose (*Primula vulgaris*); meadow saxifrage (*Saxifraga granulata*)
MOWING AND CARE In mild winters when grass grows, mow in very early spring, otherwise leave until flowers have faded and seeded, and foliage died back; then mow regularly to about 3.5cm (1¼in).

Alternatively, take a brush-cutter to the dead stems (except for the ornamental grasses) and cut them back for the winter.

There are firms worldwide that sell wildflower seed mixtures, some consisting only of native plants, some of international species. If you prepare the ground as for a conventional lawn, you can sow seed. If you intend to supplement an existing lawn, you will usually get more success with raising the seeds in a nursery bed, thereby getting sturdy young plants that will then stand a much better chance of survival when planted into the grass. You could raise your own plants from seed collected locally but take only small amounts so as not to rob the natural ecosystem.

RIGHT **Spring into summer with meadow plants, including bluebell (*Hyacinthoides hispanica*), columbine (*Aquilegia vulgaris*), Jacob's ladder (*Polemonium caeruleum*) and the pink flowers of *Nomocharis farreri*.**

FLOWER-STUDDED, WILDFLOWER LAWN

Medium-high plants flowering from early to midsummer. Can be used as a conventional lawn after flowers have died down.

SELECTED PLANTS bugle (*Ajuga reptans*); yarrow (*Achillea millifolium*); daisy (*Bellis perennis*); lady's bedstraw (*Galium verum*); field woodrush (*Luzula campestris*); hoary plantain (*Plantago media*); primrose (*Primula vulgaris*); self-heal (*Prunella vulgaris*)

MOWING AND CARE **Mow to 4cm (1½in) until early summer; after flowering mow as normal.**

HIGH SUMMER, WILDFLOWER GRASSLANDS

Taller plants for midsummer when the late grasses are also flowering.

SELECTED PLANTS yarrow (*Achillea millifolium*); columbine (*Aquilegia*); knapweed (*Centaurea scabiosa*); pignut (*Conopodium majus*); wild carrot (*Daucus carota*); American helenium (*Helenium autumnale*); day lilies (*Hemerocallis flava* and *H. fulva*); scabious (*Knautia arvensis*)

MOWING AND CARE **Mow with blades high from early until late spring, then leave for plants to develop and flower. Strim and mow.**

TALL, LATE-SUMMER PRAIRIE

Tall flowers in high waving grasses.

SELECTED PLANTS astilbe (*Astilbe chinensis*) in moist places; purple cone flower (*Echinacea purpurea*); globe thistle (*Echinops ritro*); Joe Pye weed (*Eupatorium purpureum*); miscanthus grass (*Miscanthus sinensis*); royal fern (*Osmunda regalis*); meadow rues (*Thalictrum* – European and US species)

MOWING AND CARE **Nurse plants for first 2–3 years until sturdy enough to compete with grass. Mow paths around groups of plants. Cut stems down in winter after seeding or in spring.**

MEADOWS AND PRAIRIES FOR ALL SEASONS

You can enjoy garden meadows from early spring until deep autumn. Whether you use native or naturalized plants, or a mixture of both, they will obey the imperative of the seasonal sequence. You can also plant for different heights, from low-growing snowdrops and wild daffodils, or cropped flowering lawns, to the rangy beauty of large clumpy plants growing alongside tall grasses with paths mown through them. Make your choice according to your needs. If you have a small garden and like to use the lawn during the summer, make a snowdrop display or add some spring wildflowers in a selected area and then mow as normal in early summer when the flowers and foliage have died back. High-summer wildflowers and prairie flowers are taller and less tidy in their growth, so for this enterprise you will need to set aside more space. Mown paths through the plants give a sense of coherence to the design within the garden as a whole. You can build up a display in a more restricted space by backing it onto a boundary hedge or an alcove within the garden.

MEADOWS FROM WINTER

The dominant model for the early spring meadow is that of the poetry of the *Romaunt of the Rose*, interpreted into visual form in medieval tapestries such as *La Dame à la Licorne* and the gorgeous *Book of Hours* and other illuminated manuscripts that have

found their way into museums all over the world. The earliest flowers to bloom in velvety winter grass, drenched with dew or whitened by frost and kept low by grazing or mowing, are the snowdrops (*Galanthus*) and winter aconite (*Eranthis hyemalis*), closely followed by early narcissi and primulas of various kinds. There are many named varieties of snowdrop but for a natural garden I feel you can do no better than the common, but beautifully proportioned and elegant, *G. nivalis*. The pink *Corydalis bulbosa* and the bright blue *Scilla* species (*S. biflora* and *S. siberica*) naturalize readily but for a natural effect it is best not to mix up too many species and colours, especially within a small space. In my opinion these small, mostly bulbous plants look their best in self-contained groupings.

The low plants that bloom earliest in the year enable those of us with quite small gardens to engage in meadow gardening, because lawns are not generally in use in this cold season. The succession of flowers can be appreciated and, after they have faded, the leaves should be allowed to replenish the bulbs or corms for the next year. The meadow area should be mown before it is required as lawn for the rest of the year. This can be done with a standard lawnmower, providing that the first mowing can be made with the blades somewhat higher than normal. Take the grass down in stages, allowing the plants to retire completely beneath the surface and remain dormant until the following year.

The coming of spring can be variable. It arrives not on a particular week or month but with the appearance of certain flowers. Daffodils act as heralds, blooming through a bright sequence of early- to late-flowering kinds. Those that are closest to the wild types are the most successful for meadow plantings and they should be planted in drifts of one kind, except for the hoop-petticoat daffodil (*Narcissus bulbocodium*), which looks its best dotted over a bank or threaded through damp short grass so the blooms twinkle engagingly through the green carpet. It needs good drainage and does not do well on heavy soils, where the first daffodils might be 'February Gold' or some other of the small *N. cyclamineus* cultivars characterized by their narrow trumpets and thrown-back sepals. They are dainty but very hardy and able to stand up to almost any weather that a cold spring can fling at them. Later, as the

RIGHT **Daffodils, snake's-head fritillary (***Fritillaria meleagris***), in both red and the white forms, and wood anemone (***Anemone nemorosa***), make a strong spring-meadow combination that is easy to establish in a damp lawn. Planted in autumn, they will begin flowering the following spring.**

weather warms, the highly scented, small-trumpet narcissus of the *N. poeticus* type fills the air with fragrance, as other spring plants such as early orchids and wild primroses come into flower.

Crocuses are plants of early spring, and the species look far more natural in grass than the stout, heavy-flowered hybrids. The blue-purple *Crocus tommasinianus* is one of the prettiest and most elegant. Slightly later to appear, *Corydalis solida*, with its dusty pink flowers and exquisitely dainty, fern-like leaves, naturalizes surprisingly well. As its foliage vanishes back beneath the soil soon after the flowers have faded, the grass can be mowed shortly afterwards. *Anemone blanda* will naturalize in lighter soils and can be grown in drifts of blue or white, pink and blue. Snake's-head fritillary (*Fritillaria meleagris*) takes well to garden meadows, especially those that are slightly damp. It thrives on heavier soils and will increase steadily in conditions to its liking.

ABOVE **A late spring meadow, with a lovely combination of the beautifully scented poet's narcissus (*Narcissus poeticus*) and naturalized camassia (*Camassia quamash*).**

LEFT **The pink *Chaerophyllum hirsutum* 'Roseum' is a choice constituent of alpine meadows that has translated to gardens, where it grows just as well in company with ox-eye daisies (*Leucanthemum vulgare*) and other late spring-flowering plants. It has the same habit of growth as cow parsley.**

EARLY SUMMER MEADOWS

Early summer is the quintessential time for the traditional ideal of the meadow. It can follow on quite naturally from the early-spring meadow garden or could occupy part of this area while the rest is close-mown. Plants that work well in an early summer meadow are cuckoo flowers (*Cardamine pratensis*), dog's-tooth violets (*Erythronium*), red campions (*Silene dioica*), cowslips (*Primula veris*) and Pasque flowers (*Pulsatilla vulgaris*). There are also the various *Veronica* species, especially the germander speedwell (*V. chamaedrys*), native all over Europe and naturalized in North America, whose captivating deep blue flowers, although tiny, glint so strongly among the green of the spring meadow grasses. Other plants that are typical of European grasslands but have spread far and wide include the purple, white and pink-flowered self-heal (*Prunella*), the bird's-foot trefoil (*Lotus corniculatus*), with its bright yellow-sunset flowers, and lady's mantle (*Alchemilla mollis*), with its velvety leaves.

Most of these plants are quite small and after flowering and fruiting will disappear from view, while others such as germander speedwell, lady's mantle and the trefoils will continue to grow through the summer. They will, however, not be harmed by a midsummer (or slightly later) mowing. For the rather longer grass and slightly taller plants a large rotary lawnmower should be adequate, although a strimmer, scythe or sickle could also be used. You could take the level down in stages or cut it all at once. The remaining grass will recover its greenness within a few weeks – or less if there is a good rainfall. You can allow this lawn to remain as slightly longer turf, in which case you will get a reflowering of some of the species, but it should not be allowed to grow long or the meadow plants will be stifled.

SUMMER MEADOWS

As summer advances the grass element of the meadow grows taller and the flowers of high summer grow along with it. There are several members of the pea family, such as the goat's rue (*Galega officinalis*), which can have white or lilac-purple flowers, and bush vetch (*Vicia cracca*). The tree lupin (*Lupinus arboreus*) has naturalized in other countries and is grown in some drier gardens with light soil; the garden lupins and the Canadian lupin (*Lupinus nootkatensis*) have also naturalized, while *L. perennis* of the American grasslands is beginning to be available from nurseries elsewhere. Yarrow (*Achillea millefolium*), ox-eye daisy (*Leucanthemum vulgare*), the sky-blue chicory (*Cichorium intybus*) and wild carrot (*Daucus carota*) are widespread as native and naturalized grassland plants. The deep-blue flowers of meadow clary (*Salvia pratensis*) makes a welcome show in European meadows, although it is extremely unwelcome in American states such as California, where it is banned. There is a native American prairie salvia, the blue sage (*Salvia azurea*), that has, as it scientific name suggests, paler sky-blue flowers. This species grows naturally from northern Nebraska and Minnesota to the southern states of Kentucky and Texas and is used as a late-season participant in summer wildflower meadows.

A summer meadow is typically dotted with plants of different colours and you can plant a variety of these more robust individuals at intervals over the area. In a garden setting, however, I think it is desirable to have a theme, matching the numerous colours and building up the texture. To some extent the meadow will sort itself out over time, and you will see what likes to grow for you and be able to try new plants to set up the effects you want.

In my garden columbines (*Aquilegia vulgaris*) grow strongly and self-seed and I am experimenting with growing blue and purple kinds of *Iris sibirica* with the columbines in my summer meadow. A very attractive, semi-double form of the vigorous, naturalized soapwort or bouncing Bet (*Saponaria*

BELOW The common spotted orchid of Europe and Asia (*Dactylorhiza fuchsii*) is a plant of limestone meadows, with bottle-brush flower spikes. The sturdier, robust marsh orchid (*Dactylorhiza elata*) likes more acidic conditions. The flower colour can vary from almost white to purple.

officinalis) is another favourite and it made a heady combination when it self-seeded beside a bush of *Cotinus* 'Grace', sending its pale pink flowers up through the shrub's broad, purple leaves, and setting them off to perfection.

An added pleasure of the summer meadow is the amount and variety of invertebrate life that it attracts, including moths, butterflies and many gloriously coloured bugs and insects. The large, platelike flowerheads of carrot, yarrow and other umbelliferous plants are particularly inviting to insect visitors in my garden.

The summer meadow will require a fairly heavy-duty strimmer or a lawnmower with reciprocating blades to make an effective cut. Cutting immediately after flowering can be done if you wish to restore the garden to mown neatness for the later summer and autumn. For this kind of meadow it is best to mow to a grass height of about 10cm (4in), so that the meadow is tidy but not shorn and yet short enough to keep the grasses from forming heavy clumps (except for ornamental reasons).

LEFT **Wild carrot flowerheads open in a characteristic bowl shape, often with a single crimson floret at the very centre. It is a summer plant of dusty hot meadows. The lacy flowers are attractive to a wide range of colourful insects, such as shield bugs and soldier beetles.**

BELOW **A high-summer meadow: tall ox-eye daisies with cocksfoot (*Dactylis glomerata*) and a mown path leading to a gate spanned by an apple arch, made from two single-stemmed trees trained together. The doves will enjoy the ripened seed of the grasses and meadow flowers.**

FLOWERING LAWNS

The lure of the lawn, despite being labour-intensive and prone to problems, remains strong but even if, for reasons of space or social use, you decide to retain it this need not stop you growing meadow flowers. There is quite a wide range of plants that live and sometimes flower in low grass. They are mostly plants that used to grow originally by tracks and waysides, and whose seeds are often carried by passing animals or people. One such plant, the broad-leaved plantain (*Plantago major*), was named 'white man's foot' by native Americans and, although this invasive weed is unlikely to be a plant you would seek to establish, the hoary plantain (*P. media*) is an asset in calcareous ground, with its soft broad leaves and powder-pink flowerheads.

The best-known lawn plant is the ubiquitous daisy, the herald both of summer and daybreak. To those who worship the flawless lawn that is incapable of survival except with intensive care in terms of cutting, fertilizing and pesticides, it is considered a weed, along with buttercups (*Ranunculus*), self-heal (*Prunella*) and clovers (although it seems to me that a spirit of tolerance should be shown). All gardens are different and it may be that one particular species (sometimes an unlikely candidate) will begin to dominate; if this proliferation is not to your taste you may have to take control measures. The pretty blue speedwell (*Veronica filiformis*), originally introduced to gardens as an ornamental, escaped in Britain in 1927, and in the last decade or so has established itself vigorously in lawns in Britain and the USA. Garden speedwell (*V. longifolia*), native in European gardens, has naturalized in North American lawns and banks. However, unless the intruder gives real offence, it can be more rewarding to keep a watching brief and observe how the dynamics of the flower lawn changes in successive years.

Much depends on the personal tastes and tolerances of the gardener. The little shade-loving evergreen helxine (*Soleirolia soleirolii*) does not grow for me, but I know people whose shaded lawns are overrun with it. Some of these gardeners are in despair at the failure of their efforts to stop the incomer; while others have decided that after all, since grass never grew strongly in the shade, the helxine is green, attractive and preferable. It has to be said, however, that a natural garden is luxuriant in its growth but it has an essential order rather than a disregard for neglect. Rampant weeds are as untidy and out of place in a garden of natural style as in any other, and as much of a nuisance.

RIGHT Give a lawn its head for just a few weeks and it may well surprise you. Even common plants such as buttercups and a few bluebells can look glorious, as here with a small rocky outcrop and sinuous beds, usually associated with close-cropped lawns. It can be restored to neat lawn with very little difficulty when the flowers and foliage die back.

BELOW A welcome arrival in a lawn. Shaggy inkycap mushrooms (*Coprinus comatus*) do no damage. Watch them turn from pristine whiteness to inky deliquescence or pick them early to eat on toast.

OPPOSITE Some cultivated tulips will continue to bloom reliably in a meadow, providing soil conditions are suitable. Ideally, they like a light, well-drained soil in a sunny place. A few especially tough varieties of tulip, such as the old-fashioned, red 'Apeldoorn', will bloom even in heavy, wetter soils.

PRAIRIE MEADOWS

The crown for the most flamboyant, late-summer plants has to go to the flora of North America. However, although the showy prairie plants that thrilled the first settlers have been used extensively in meadow landscapes over the last century, Europeans were unenthusiastic about using prairie plants until fairly recently. Some plants were brought over to Europe from the USA in colonial times and given local names – such as New England aster (*Aster novae-angliae*) was adopted as Michaelmas daisy – while some names given by the American settlers were taken over, including spiderwort (*Tradescantia*) and golden rod (*Solidago*). However, of the more recently appreciated plants are still called by their scientific generic names in Europe (rudbeckias, heleniums, echinaceas and gauras, for example).

True prairies, like other kinds of meadow, have at least eighty percent or more grass species in their composition, which means that the bold, bright colours of the late-flowering plants are muted by the green and gold matrix of stems and grass flowerheads. This is not the impression that the American wildflower catalogues convey. Some of their seed mixtures contain no grasses at all and often include annuals and introductions. The would-be prairie gardener has an initial choice to make:

whether to play true to the original concept and plant grasses with a roughly correct proportion of wildflowers; or to aim for a meadow-prairie effect without the grasses; or to compromise, perhaps planting a select few of these beautiful clumping plants into an existing summer meadow to extend the season. The choice will depend on personal taste, as well as the amount of space that can be allocated to the project and the use that will be made of the meadow area. The romance of the mid-western prairie, to my mind, cannot be summoned up in miniature; it calls for something of the spaciousness and the grand scale of the original.

Making a selection of American wildflowers that have proved themselves in gardens is another matter. Some, such as asters and golden rod, have already adopted themselves into the natural landscapes of other countries, while others such as Joe Pye weed (*Eupatorium purpurea*), cone flowers (*Echinacea*), helianthemums, penstemons, blazing star (*Liatris*) and bergamot (*Monarda fistulosa*) have become familiar garden plants all over the temperate world. These, and many others that are becoming more readily available away from their native continent, can be grown in groupings or planted as individuals into existing meadows. One of the advantages of the more robust prairie plants is that they grow both vigorously and quickly and are able to out-compete weed species.

A few late-season European plants call for a place: hemp agrimony, the counterpart to Joe Pye weed, has pink rather than purple flowers and green not purplish foliage; nor is it so burly, but it is still a good plant for meadows with a certain amount of dampness. For drier sites the globe thistle (*Echinops*), with hazy-blue prickly balls of flowers, is robust enough to survive among grasses, as well as in groupings without grass competition. Scabious (*Knautia* and *Scabiosa*) are attractive late-season meadow plants with blue-lilac flowers, and the purple devil's-bit scabious (*Succisa pratensis*), the latest flowering of all, is certainly an asset. Knapweeds (*Centaurea*) in crimson-purples are a widespread genus, similar in appearance to thistles and very attractive to butterflies and other insects.

LEFT **An American, annual wildflower seed mixture growing to splendid effect in a small garden. Mainly Californian and Shirley poppies (*Eschscholzia californica* and *Papaver rhoeas*), this blend may self-seed, but the ground will need cultivating each autumn.**

LEFT The large-flowered aster hybrids will not actually self-seed like the species, but they will persist for years in the right conditions, a pleasure to both people and to butterflies.

PLANTING PLAN FOR A PRAIRIE MEADOW

A prairie border can be concentrated into a smaller area than the more open, grassy prairie meadow and it is more colourful and densely planted. Much of the planting is taken from the beautiful, late-flowering species of North America, but in the prairie border, they are augmented by other larger, late-season flowering plants and grasses that make good clumps or drifts.

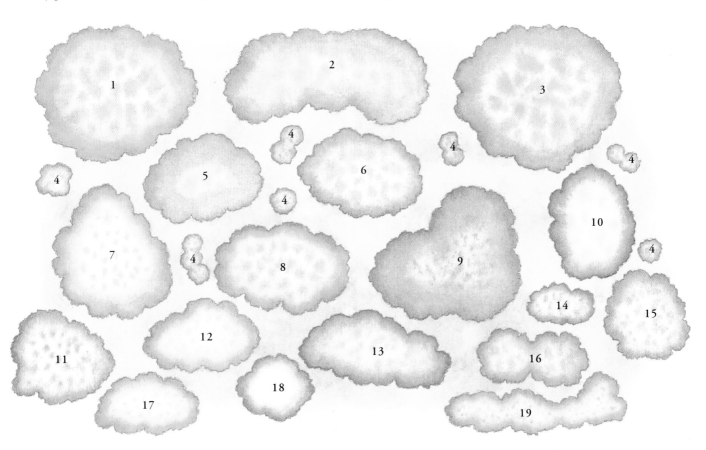

KEY TO PLANTING

1 Joe Pye weed *Eupatorium purpureum*
2 Grass *Miscanthus sinensis* 'Malepartus'
3 Queen of the prairies *Filipendula rubra*
4 *Verbena bonariensis*
5 Indian grass *Sorghastrum nutans*
6 *Sanguisorba obtusa*
7 *Echinacea purpurea* 'White Lustre'

8 Purple cone flower *Echinacea purpurea*
9 Switch grass *Panicum virgatum*
10 Meadowsweet *Filipendula ulmaria*
11 Globe thistle *Echinops ritro* 'Veitch's Blue'
12 *Astrantia major*
13 Grass *Pennisetum orientale*
14 *Scabiosa caucasica*

15 Knapweed *Centaurea nigra*
16 *Astilbe* 'Jo Ophorst'
17 Musk mallow *Malva moschata*
18 *Gaura lindheimeri*
19 Meadow cranesbill *Geranium pratense*

PRAIRIE BORDERS

Prairie borders are groupings of prairie plants without the grass matrix, and are therefore more colourful and densely planted than you would ever find in the wild state. In effect they constitute a bold, late-season border that is rather less labour-intensive than the traditional border. It is possible to make a good border of this kind in a purist sense using only North American prairie plants but some of these are difficult to come by or to grow away from their native habitat, and a prairie border can be attractively augmented with other late-season selections. Grasses in these borders are planted not as a green matrix but as stars in their own right. There are some handsome authentic prairie grasses that look lovely with asters or golden rod. One of the most beautiful is switch grass (*Panicum virgatum*) with its diffuse arcs of tiny bead-like flowers. It is a tall plant (up to 2m (6ft)) and easy going, thriving even in poorer soils as long as it has full sun. Allow plenty of room also for the graceful, fine-textured Indian grass or wood grass (*Sorghastrum nutans*), which also likes full sun and prefers a reasonably fertile soil, growing between 1–2m (3–6ft) and producing late-season, elegantly falling flower panicles.

In a more eclectic grouping, *Miscanthus*, with their arching silky panicles, are among the most beautiful and reliable of grasses. They need full sun and usually do better in slightly moist conditions, although they will not tolerate being waterlogged in winter. Sedges, too, can play a part, with smaller ones at the edge of the border or taller ones, such as the easy-going, pendulous sedge (*Carex pendula*), a robust plant that reaches 1m (3ft) or a little more, and has strong stems and pendent, green-brown flowerheads that resemble heavy late-summer catkins, further into the border.

A prairie border can be planted to have the stepped effect of a conventional border or given more natural-looking mix-and-match groupings with different heights and colours. The danger is trying to pack together too many plants and losing the sense of individual form. If you pick and choose from different parts of the world, you also need to keep an aesthetic sense of what will combine gracefully with the other plants or there will be a jarring of colour and shapes. Overall, the prairie meadow is a generous, open-ended kind of gardening, where personal taste and gradually gained experience of what kinds of plant take more readily to your garden conditions make it a most exciting and experimental style.

Bold perennial plants that grow in eye-catching clumps interact with the dramatic grasses within the prairie border. Some of the rich-coloured prairie

LEFT **A fanfare of summer colours, with wild, naturalized and cultivated flowers in managed abandon: lupins, marigolds, red poppies, mulleins, sunflowers, *Verbena bonariensis*, tiger lilies and hibiscus all vie for attention.**

plants set the tone: the red-purple species (*Echinacea purpurea*) or cultivars such as *E. p.* 'Robert Bloom', which has a touch more crimson. Joe Pye weed (*Eupatorium purpureum*) and the stiff, purple candelabra flowerheads of *Verbena hastata*, both striking and individual plants, add depth and richness of colour to the border. Foxgloves, for midsummer and thistles (*Eryngium* or *Centaurea*, for example) later in the season can be interspersed between the larger plants. The effect is lifted with plants by pale-toned plants such as *Lysimachia ephemerum* with its pale tall spires, or clouds of white-flowered *Crambe cordifolia* in midsummer, while the dense, tight, creamy spearheads of *Veronicastrum virginicum* and *Verbascum chaixii* flower from late summer into autumn. Purple-leaved cotinus or evergreens such as bamboos, holly or box, can be used to create a foliage backdrop. Holly or box, lightly clipped, adds a formal note that emphasizes the exuberance of the rest of the border.

LEFT A damp meadow in the western USA with native species on a sunny June day, showing the yellow, daisy-like flowers known over there as mule's ears, and scarlet *Gilia*. These are both plants that like a moist soil and full sun.

BELOW Grasses are perhaps at their most dramatic when planted on their own. Here, the grasses *Stipa* and *Miscanthus*, planted with bamboo, create an extravagant effect in a woodland clearing.

USING A NATURAL GARDEN

A garden with natural style should be an inviting place, somewhere for those who use it to enjoy and where there is always something of interest. It is a place to grow herbs or pick home-grown fruit through the seasons, where children play and cats and dogs can chase or doze peacefully – but also where adults can relax and be tranquil, under a green canopy of trees or beside a pool. You can take work outdoors, give yourself a quiet break, entertain a large party – or walk quietly at any time from dawn till dusk. You can use your garden to extend an interest in sculpture, design, plant life or natural history at your own pace.

OPPOSITE **An informal kitchen garden in late summer, with beehives and plants that include sunflowers, broccoli, onions and herbs. The flowering herbs and hyssop are good bee plants, while the beans in flower also have their pollinators close by.**

DECORATIVE ELEMENTS

Gardening in a natural way used to be associated with frugality and a rather rough and basic effect. The last decade or so has seen a complete change in attitude, because people have come to see that a philosophy which recognizes the importance of conserving resources and working with natural forces is not only practical but also stylish. Even compost bins have been given a new look, designed with elegance and distinction and for more better efficiency, and incorporated into garden plans by well-respected garden designers.

It cannot be said too strongly that a garden which adopts a natural style is not a wild and disorderly garden. On the contrary, a garden that is overgrown and out of control contains a smaller number of habitats, attracts less wildlife and sustains fewer plant species, because the burly ones overwhelm the less robust ones and create a dominant habitat. The art of the natural garden is to identify and develop each of the natural habitats and to maintain them at their

optimum. This way it will support and invite a greater range of plants and animals and will also be a pleasure to the people who use it.

The modern style that developed from the passion for wilflower gardening in the USA and Europe (especially The Netherlands), and the recognition of the value of indigenous flora in Australia and New Zealand, has adopted a wider range of plants, although it also uses them in new ways. A sense of design is realized in a naturalistic style that includes ornamentation and works of art. The process continues as gardeners discover new plants that are prepared to naturalize (helped in some cases by changing climatic conditions) and explore different ways of using them, while alongside, new and rediscovered forms of garden art complement the planting. There is enormous scope for ideas that understand the need of environmentally conscious gardeners with smaller gardens – ideas that blend nature and artifice.

Some of the most beautiful sculpture of recent decades is made in organic materials. Ornamental driftwoods and pieces in hardwood will last, while many other modern sculptures made from less stable materials will decay *in situ* and eventually be blown away by the wind or reincorporated into the earth. The elegant willow sculptures may last for many years; the poetry of leaf sculpture will vanish with the season; the beautiful water patterns created by water sculptors are lasting, although they will change with weather conditions and the seasons.

Paths, internal and external boundaries, lighting and social areas, and their integration one with another, all play a role within an informally relaxed but handsome garden design. The garden should in the final assessment seem neither sloppily lax nor overstretched with too many fiddly details and an excess of planting. Ideally, it should seem perfectly appropriate to its setting, full of life and promise.

BELOW **Found items, such as logs and driftwood, make good decoration within a natural-style garden. Here, a certain amount of art has contrived a rare European alligator that slithers and slides from the undergrowth.**

OPPOSITE **Where an artefact such as a sundial draws the eye, the surrounding planting seems to compose itself around it. Hardy geraniums and astrantia set the tone for this early summer scene, with the small, bright carmine European gladiolus making splashes of rich colour.**

DECORATIVE PROJECTS

The old art of working with living trees has been rediscovered, and gardens again are being ornamented with skilfully made arbours, and by trained fruit trees and bushes, espaliered apples and pears, globe-headed gooseberry bushes, and innovatory shapes, such as step-over apple trees that can act as a fruit-bearing edging to a potager or mixed bed. Espaliers are both a controlled way of introducing additional varieties of fruit into a smaller garden as well as a beautiful and productive living trellis.

Arbours provide shelter and seating in a garden, and they can also reflect a dominant mood. You introduce a sense of solidity and permanence with the velvety dark foliage of yew, a cheerful brightness with hawthorn, and almost instant shelter with fast-growing species such as willow.

In researching this book I was intrigued to notice that arbours receive no mention in several of the most compendious and comprehensive gardening dictionaries and companions. In the illustrated books, modern arbours consisted of heavy metal structures, beams lightly dusted with wisterias or, in one case, a very solid, wooden-arched affair with a

ridiculous conglomeration of roses perched on top like a wedding hat. There were examples of other structures in willow and hazel, twined more or less successfully with climbing plants. In other words, we seem temporarily to have lost sight of the original conception of the arbour, which was primarily a curious interweaving of living plants.

The medieval period was full of such arbours, some of them taking their inspiration from the gardening writings of Pietro Crescenzi from early in the fourteenth century, in which he described how to 'plant fruit-bearing trees which can be easily interlaced, such as cherries and apple trees; or else olives or poplars which will grow quickly'. Sometimes these living arbours were themselves interplanted with scented climbing plants; in Shakespeare's *Much Ado About Nothing*, Beatrice is to go to the 'pleached bower/Where honeysuckles ripened by the sun/Forbid the sun to enter'. These would create an inviting shade in hot climates, where one needed respite from a persecuting sun, but in cooler climates arbours might be south-facing, presenting a warm place to sit and rest in pleasant

BELOW **The skills that create beautiful and functional willow baskets can be turned to art in willow sculptures. These woven-willow geese grazing a garden lawn are full of life. The hurdle fence in the background is functional as well as attractive.**

HOW TO MAKE AN ARBOUR

Hawthorn can make a densely textured arbour that will be private and fairly windproof. Willow gives quicker, more latticed results but will require more trimming. An even more rapid finish can be achieved by making a trellis framework and covering it with ivy. The little extra time and effort involved in using hawthorn is worthwhile as it will stay crip, need little maintenance and last for many years.

1 Plant 12 hawthorn (*Crataegus monogyna*) bare-rooted whips (small trees) in autumn, three for each side, six along the back, about 40cm (16in) apart. Stake with 2m (6ft) bamboos. Treat as for a hedge, trimming at intervals until they grow to the required height, and trim.

2 During winter, secure a bamboo scaffolding along the top of the arbour and let the leading shoots grow up. After autumn leaf-fall, bend the pliable shoots over, weave them together and tie them in.

3 During the next season let the leaders grow (upwards or at an angle), until all meet across the top of the arbour when brought to the horizontal. Tie them in and trim. Continue to trim and clip until the arbour is to your satisfaction. Thereafter trim twice a year.

ABOVE You do not need a degree in willow sculpture to enjoy making garden structures. Here, willow branches, taken from pollard prunings, have been used to made a pleasant leafy arbour. All that needs to be done is to set the willow branches into the ground – and wait.

dappled shade. When 'dead wood' was specified for construction, it was for the rapid result that would ensue, as climbing plants quickly smothered it.

Willow arbours grow very quickly from stems set into the ground and, as Crescenzi says, their pliable shoots can be easily woven or bound together. They do not, however, stop growing when the arbour has been fashioned, and people with willow arbours must be prepared to keep on top of the weaving and pruning. Hawthorn is a traditional subject for arbours (*see p.99*), and once established makes a dense textures of twigs, small leaves and flowers. In Britain, arbours of this kind have been created at Hatfield House in Hertfordshire and need only light trimming a few times each year.

To achieve an arbour of this sort, you plant as for a hedge but in the shape of an open oblong – the long side stretching far enough to accommodate the bench that will eventually be placed within, and with slightly curving wings each side of it. Be patient while the plants form a root system capable of sustaining the upward growth and, as the plants rise, trim them to shape. In the final stages you can leave the top open or bring them over in a shell-like curve, depending on the amount of sun and light you desire.

Do not entirely despise constructions made of 'dead wood', however, especially when used on a smaller scale. Useful supports for paeonies are best made from stout, twiggy branches, placed to make a crown around the growing plant, so that they support the foliage and flowers as they mature. Rustic but elegant supports for sweet peas, clematis and runner beans can be made from a wigwam of longer hazel or willow branches about 2m (8ft) long, the lower parts firmly lodged in the soil, the upper parts held in place with woven willow or raffia ties.

BELOW **Fairly formal garden ornaments, such as statues and urns, have an extra charm when placed within a slightly informal setting. Here, the longer grass and billowing roses create a perfect descant to the classical urn on its plinth.**

ABOVE **Attention to detail is well worthwhile. A wigwam support need not be starkly utilitarian but a pleasure in itself. Such a structure can be bought or made from trimmed branches, lightly woven together and secured with pliable young hazel or willow twigs, or with raffia.**

OPPOSITE **Roses are not usually reckoned to have a decorative value in wintertime, but their long, pliable, whippy shoots make them idea for arches. A scented climber, such as 'Compassion', would be excellent.**

NATURAL ORNAMENTS AND ACCESSORIES

BELOW **Stone seals flecked with lichens on a sea of garden bluebells (***Hyacinthoides***), with the biogeneric hybrid x** *Fatshedera lizei* **as a backdrop. It is a good bet that the more artlessly casual the effect, the more thought has gone into the placing of a sculpture.**

On first consideration, one might imagine that sculpture and garden artefacts, such as sundials, bird baths, or even garden furniture, would be out of place in a natural style of garden. In practice, art in many forms works exceptionally well. This means not simply the rounded, weathered-look natural shapes of a Henry Moore or Barbara Hepworth sculpture, but also more formal works. Even if the surrounding vegetation has become a little overgrown, the presence of an artefact at a strategic point gives an impression of convergence, so it appears to be an intentional composition. Sometimes a rock fashioned in a striking shape will make a considerable impact on its own as a natural sculpture. In my region of southeastern

England, rock is scarce and people have for centuries cherished the few large pieces: sandstone sarsens brought in during the ice age, and a kind of prehistoric cemented rock, known as puddingstone, that consists of pebbles trapped together in a silicate matrix. They may be found in fairly large pieces that in the past were incorporated into sacred shrines and church walls, but are also given pride of place in gardens. Flint is our commonest stone, and it makes lovely walls, especially when used with local brick. There are a few sculptors who have combined and knapped the obdurate flints to make pieces of considerable flair. The ideal might be to find exactly the right piece of sculpture at an exhibition or even

to commission one. Good works sometimes turn out to be less expensive than might be thought. There are outdoor galleries devoted entirely to artworks for the garden, and some of the big auction houses (Sotheby's, for example) have dedicated sales grounds, while many galleries and auctions have occasional garden works up for sale. Even if you don't buy, these are both interesting and fun to walk around, and their catalogues make a useful aide-mémoire of garden artefacts. The works of art include everything imaginable, from small items of sculpture to huge statues or well-heads, as well as benches, stone and iron balustrades and topiary.

It is, however, possible to find nice things, even on a very limited budget. If you choose carefully, you can discover interesting and well-made garden artefacts at garden centres and stores. In a local garden warehouse I found a small stone frog for my own pond, superior to many at several times the price. It is also well worth looking in at architectural and builders' salvage yards – you can often find articles in stone, wood and metal in these collections. It is astonishing what ingenuity and good materials can inspire in people. I am continually amazed at the creativity of friends and acquaintances: shallow water stairs out of old encaustic tiles; a small fountain head pieced together from different pieces of stone; a chequer-board herb garden out of a job-lot of square blocks of limestone. There are wonderful fountains

ABOVE **This statue plays a key role in the nuttery, with the plants beneath chosen for spring-flowering and illuminating lime-green coloration:** *Smyrnium perfoliatum*; *Euphorbia amygdaloides* var. *robbiae*, **Bowles' golden grass (***Milium effusum* 'Aureum'**), wood anemones, sweet woodruff (***Galium odoratum***), and** *Trillium sessile.*

LEFT **Ceramic deva houses, situated in order to attract nearby divine spirits, are here set among the gently toned flowers of a Californian herb garden, with its mullein spires and salvia flowers.**

LEFT There are very few sculptors prepared to work in such an obdurate material as flint. This figure, created by Peter Goven, is one of many works he has created in flint, thereby proving that a respect for the nature of a material can stimulate remarkable and unusual artistic results.

BELOW The sculptor William Pye combines a skill with works of art that involve water with a sense of what suits gardens of different types. His water sculpture 'Water Trellis', with its lattice of fine spouts, makes a delightful composition with these mounded grey-green plants.

made of huge driftwood trunks by Daryl Stokes, a sculptor in Monterey, California, in which copper bowls have been inserted with water splashing from one to the other.

You may feel that statuary and urns have too strong an echo of classical gardens. If this kind of ornamentation seems out of place in your garden, consider a distinctive artefact that is both useful and a focal point, such as a well-crafted seat. Even if you are rarely at rest, an elegantly-proportioned, well-made seat at a critical area of the garden will always be a pleasure to look at, and may at some stage induce you to take advantage of it and take your ease.

Recent years have seen a brilliant exploitation of art made from organic materials, such as leaves, twigs, berries and old pieces of wood. Variations on the theme include patterns in pebbles and rocks and forms made from small pieces of limestone flakes, slate or tile. Sculptures in willow shoots are woven into tremendous flowing figures and animals. A contemplative maze can be made on a small lawn, with close-mown or gravel paths, which can be walked along slowly as they wind to the centre.

OPPOSITE A small dovecote can be seen through this tumble of Canadian golden rod (*Solidago canadensis*), Shasta daisies (*Leucanthemum* x *superbum*) and evening primrose (*Oenothera biennis*), within a conifer clearing.

ENTERTAINING AND LIGHTING

There can be fewer pleasures more complete than entertaining friends in a garden setting. Food seems more delicious, conversation more interesting – and the world an altogether better place out of doors, amid the flowers and foliage. I cherish the memory of a breakfast in the glimmering winter sun on New Year's day on the balcony of a rented house near the Mediterranean coast; although in cool-temperate climates, the number of months during which you can eat outdoors is limited. This makes the experience all the more precious, and you must be sure to cultivate an approach to outdoor living and dining that will not impede your enjoyment.

While I enjoy picnics as much as anybody, I feel that these are for travelling abroad, or days out. At home, I like to eat at a table. There is a lot of well-made, well-designed garden furniture on offer, but while there is no shortage of choice, you need to make sure it is the right size and style for your garden. You do not, for example, want to wrestle with heavy furniture each time a meal outdoors takes your fancy, nor is it pleasant to watch expensive purchases deteriorating before your eyes, because they are exposed to the weather. Some garden furniture is designed to be left outdoors – certain hardwoods look better after a few years than they did when new, as the weathering process modifies the colour. It would, however, be a pity if gardens in the Western world were promoting natural style at the expense of tropical forests, so it is important to check that such furniture is made from timber grown in properly managed forests.

BELOW **A flowery grove of columbines with meadow grass, Welsh poppies and garden angelica in a wooded alcove, with presiding bust, where you could equally well relax with a drink, take a pile of work, or simply enjoy the sights and sounds of the garden.**

Cast-iron and aluminium furniture will last many years as long as you make sure the paint is in reasonably good condition and chips are quickly covered. Powder coating has meant that the surfaces are very well protected, so usually it is only light touching-up that is necessary. If the design is good, garden furniture can itself be a pleasure to look at, a kind of sculpture you can use. It also has to be comfortable, so try it as thoroughly as possible before you buy. I like to have matching chairs, some of which can be placed independently in other parts of the garden to catch the best weather or which can be augmented with folding chairs for a bigger party.

Sitting under a tree, so that the table is at least partly shaded is usually a good bet, although in our garden the cats like to join the outdoor party, considering it good fun to climb about in the tree while we are eating and to knock blossom, apples or leaves down upon on us. Where you put the table should also be determined by the quality of the view over the garden, and by how far you have to bring tableware and food. The golden rule for outdoor eating is to keep it simple.

Cooking outdoors is another matter, but is made easier by the advent of very good portable barbecues. The simplest of these are Vietnamese cast-iron pots, with a grid over the top to cook on. For those who make a habit of cooking outdoors, there are some excellent designs for permanent outdoor cooking fixtures in brick, with a chimney to draw off the smoke, places for the ashes, and a compartment where you store wood and other extras. If it is to be permanent, it is worth taking a bit of trouble with both the design and execution.

Hammocks can be hung from trees, walls or free-standing posts. The South American type, made of an intricate lattice of fine string, must be one of the most therapeutic products ever conceived. You lie sideways in them and they can accommodate one or two people. The gentle swinging to and fro is deliciously soothing, and they are comfortable enough to sleep in overnight. Hammocks look more attractive than deck-chairs or sun-loungers and take up less room when stored. It is a good plan to make the fixings for them permanent. These need not be obtrusive: a rope fixing tied to a metal hook or a coach bolt driven securely into a stout wall.

If you do not have a convenient tree to provide shade or wish to provide a shady spot on a terrace, consider a large umbrella or parasol. Canvas kinds come in a variety of beautiful shapes, and last for

years if stored carefully during the winter. Less expensive but just as attractive, the oriental waxed parasols are elegant and effective. They tear quite easily but last well if you are careful of them. They can also give temporary respite from the sun and glare in a hot conservatory – a situation out of the wind, and one where you do not have to watch out for the parasol billowing like a sail and taking wing.

GIVING PARTIES

It is pleasant to allow parties to spill out from the house or conservatory into the garden, especially if you have a terrace or courtyard where people can linger and talk. A party that extends into the night demands the safe lighting of paths and steps, and romantic illumination elsewhere to keep other areas of the garden dreamily leafy and mysterious.

Some people go to elaborate lengths to wire up their gardens in order to play music everywhere. Apart from the possible nuisance to neighbours, this seems unnecessarily intrusive. For my taste, the quiet of the garden should beckon from the brighter, noisier reaches of the house and allow the party-goer to enjoy outdoor sounds: the hoots, rustles and subliminal squeaks of wildlife in the garden at night.

Perhaps we should adopt something of the conviviality of past designs, when gardens were designed as social places. In contrast to depictions of present-day gardens, which often seem isolated and devoid of humanity, gardens in history always show people enjoying themselves, walking the *allées* and admiring the rare plants.

ABOVE **A Canadian** *fête champêtre* **(outdoor party) near Quebec. Created by the sculptor Charles Smith, this jazz quartet makes an amusing contribution to a garden where a short growing season surely makes its owners appreciate the value of the days they are able to spend out of doors.**

RIGHT **A typical pathside light. Such lights often come in sets of four or six, with a low-voltage transformer. There is usually the possibility of adding extra lights if you have a long garden. Lighting such as this is easy to install, cheap to run and repair, and represents very good value.**

BELOW **A charming and well-made brass Indian lantern. This type of lantern can be hung individually in trees or on hooks, and is lit by a brass 'candle' that holds liquid fuel and burns with a steady flame. Alternatively, these lamps can be electrically powered and installed in sets.**

LIGHTING

Lighting is important for people whose working life keeps them away for most of the day, and for whom garden illumination extends the opportunity of enjoying the garden into late evenings in summer and autumn. Lighting is also essential in terms of safety and security. Nothing keeps out would-be burglars so usefully as lights, and they are essential in illuminating the way down paths at night time. Lights also give you a garden view even if you do not actually venture outdoors.

There is more to lighting the garden than utilitarianism, however. Moonlight brings a different kind of texture and surface reality to plants. Light from the moon may be strong enough to cast shadows and dapple the ground, but it is of a magical quality, entirely transforming the known garden. The moon is only bright enough to create its effects occasionally each month, but I think that subtle illumination of the garden can and should aspire to the same quality of light.

The low-level lights that are readily available at gardening stores are both effective for illuminating paths and softly discreet if hidden within or behind perennial plants so that the lights themselves are partially concealed and their beam diffused. For party use, there are delightful containers that consist of glass saucers that each holding a small candle or night-light, covered by a cut-glass shade that both keeps off the wind and gives a sparkle to the gentle and flickering light.

There are various kinds of flares and beacons available for garden use, some of which have fuel containing an insect repellent. You can find ingenuous Indian lanterns, fitted with a brass 'candle' which you fill with a special lamp oil that is odourless and smokeless (get it from a lamp shop or marine store). For an unsophisticated, impromptu effect, collect attractive multi-faceted pickle-and-jam-jars and place a candle or night-light inside.

Foliage lit from beneath looks unfamiliar and mysterious, and the pattern of twigs in winter and the subtleties of the branching of trees are shown off to their best by soft simple lights. Personally, I find floodlights overdramatic, bleaching out the subtleties of nature rather than revealing them. Smaller white lights are a different matter; during the twelve days of Christmas, I always weave a skein of white, outdoor Christmas-tree lights into the branches of the medlar tree – the effect of which is to create the most beautiful tracery, especially when there is a hoar frost.

WAYS OF LIGHTING THE GARDEN

Lighting extends your enjoyment of the garden, whether you are sitting outdoors in summer or looking out on winter tracery. Light can come from above or below, in the form of focused spots, lanterns, low voltage or brilliant security. Experiment before you install a system and be sure to follow safety procedures.

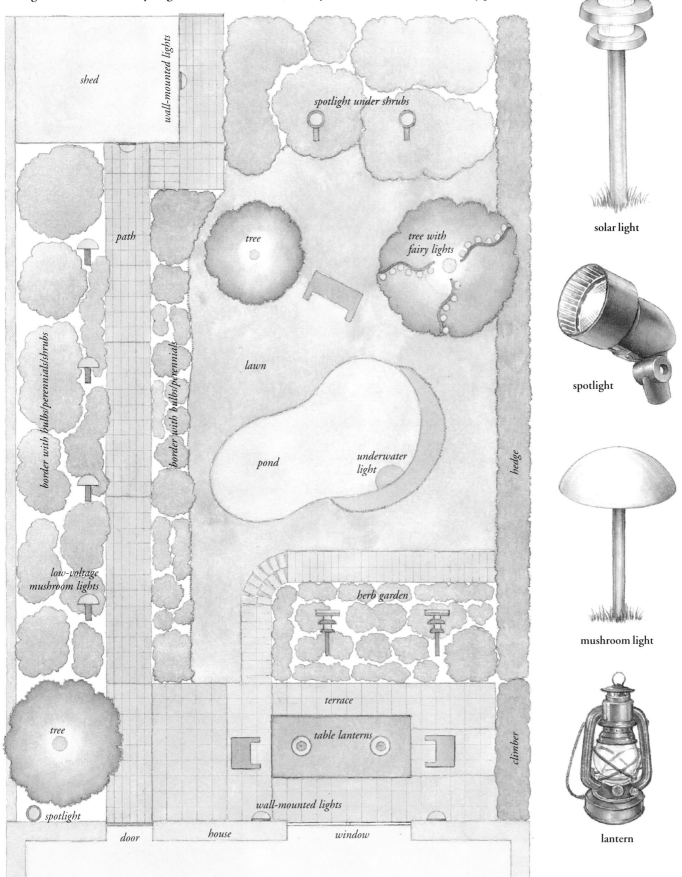

shed

wall-mounted lights

spotlight under shrubs

path

tree

tree with fairy lights

border with bulbs/perennials/shrubs

border with bulbs/perennials

lawn

hedge

pond

underwater light

low-voltage mushroom lights

herb garden

tree

terrace

table lanterns

climber

spotlight

wall-mounted lights

door   *house*   *window*

solar light

spotlight

mushroom light

lantern

FRUITS, HERBS AND SALAD GREENS

Food fresh from the garden is incomparably better than any you can find elsewhere – not only can you choose the varieties whose flavour you like best but the food is guaranteed to be absolutely fresh and pesticide free. It is much easier, too, to walk a few steps into the garden than to drive to the nearest supermarket to find vegetables that are already beginning to age. Quite apart from this, there is the pleasure and satisfaction of growing for the table, as well as the surprise in finding out how easy it is.

Despite the fact that my family seems always to be rushed for time, we always grow some salad greens and vegetables – the easy ones that will faithfully produce even if we have to neglect them a little. A strong consideration for me has always been that I knew our vegetables were pesticide-free, so I could encourage the children to eat them whenever they felt like it. As a result, they enjoy most kinds of greens and can make a pretty delicious herb and salad roll if they are stuck for a snack.

With salads, fruit and vegetables, as with non-edible plants, you match the plants you grow to soil and climate. At the very least you can add some herbs to the sunny places, and line the edge of a border with decorative lettuce plants. 'Salad Bowl' (in red or green) is one of the most ornamental of lettuces – it tastes good and a few leaves at a time may be picked from each plant, so as not to leave gaps at harvest.

Amongst other easily grown lettuces, I like the Batavia types (sometimes these have a touch of red to them) and both old and new kinds of Cos. Lettuces are very beautiful, especially when the young leaves start to mature and the sun shines through them.

I like to grow lettuces together in groups in one of my deep beds. These beds are particularly good in heavy cold soils, and are designed to be just wide enough for the gardener to be able to reach to the middle from either side. My own beds are 3.5m (11ft) long and 1.5m (5ft) wide, although these proportions may obviously be varied to suit taste and the size of your own garden. I also take advantage of the fact that the soil is turned as I sow and harvest, and plant or sow a few annuals, such as poppies, Californian poppies (*eschscholzia*), cornflowers and marigolds, among the crops. I often grow purely ornamental plants in the part of the deep bed that is close to the main path, and I have fruit bushes in some of the beds, divided from the main lawn by a row of espaliered apple trees – a design that works well and looks quite handsome.

It is surprising how much you can grow in one or two deep beds with a reasonably fertile soil, and how decorative they can look. Growing shallots from sets planted in early spring is the easiest and tastiest way to produce your own onions. They clump up in the summer in groups of reds and browns, depending on the varieties, which can range from quite sweet to sharp. There are few kinds of foliage more ornamental than that of carrots, and a row or two is essential if the soil is reasonably friable. If the soil is cold and heavy prepare it well and then choose round rather than long varieties to secure a crop. Pull them when they are young and sweet, before the pests get to them. Turnips can also be pulled young to grate in salads or lightly steam. They come in white, crimson and molten orange colours; the tops can also be eaten as a green vegetable.

Growing for yourself, there is plentiful scope to augment the standard salad greens with a range of unusual ones. American cress, or land cress, has an agreeable sharpness and lasts well into winter, while

BELOW **Ruby chard is easy to grow and tastes delicious sliced thin in salads or lightly steamed with butter. It has enjoyed a great vogue as a chic potager plant, but do not let that put you off. It is grown here with small but brilliant scarlet geraniums (*Pelargonium*), possibly 'Coddenham'.**

OPPOSITE **A glamorous kitchen garden, with vegetables and flowers neatly intermingled, the golden African marigolds blazing between the greens of the cabbage, tomato and artichoke foliage. Cosmos, dahlias, cleomes, cannas and nicotiana provide cut flowers for the house.**

corn salad is bland and slightly crunchy, teaming very well with radicchio or endive. All of these can be picked well into autumn and, if covered, often into early winter. Rocket, radishes and spring onions are quick summer crops for sunny places, while spinach, like lettuce, prefers a cooler moist soil. A small clump of sorrel will provide a piquant lemony flavour for salads and soups and, if cut down regularly, will last for several years. The recently developed small, sweet tomatoes (such as 'Sungold') make little bushes that can look quite decorative and crop furiously without the fuss that needed to be lavished on older varieties. They do appreciate a little extra water and special, high potash fertilizer but they will manage without.

As the rich foliage of courgettes, pumpkins and squashes likes to run, they need more room than most of the compact salad greens and vegetables so far described. Pumpkins are certainly worth growing, for the delicious taste of some of the smaller varieties (such as 'Hubbard' and 'Butternut'), as well as for their high nutritive value. A few shallots, some olive oil and a pumpkin will provide a memorable soup that can be made in a few minutes with the addition of either water or vegetable stock.

It is possible to run a kitchen-garden plot on natural principles if you keep the soil replenished with compost, adding a little every time you take plants out for harvest or prepare the ground for sowing or planting. The idea of deep beds is that you prepare the soil in them thoroughly by double digging to start with, but then neither dig nor tread on the soil again for several years. You do, however, need to keep the ground full of plant life, sowing or planting closer than you would in a conventional plot, a practice that also gives weeds less of a chance to invade. In the rich deep soil, weeds that do appear are easily pulled out. In my experience, growing a little of several kinds of salad greens and vegetables not only keeps me from going over my boredom threshold but deters pests to a great extent. In fact, I like walking among my fruits and vegetables just as much – if not more – than among the flowers and shrubs. It gives me great pleasure and means that, while I am enjoying the sights and scents, I notice if any plants are suffering from disease or water shortage or if there are any unwelcome pests, enabling me to take action quickly before the situation becomes serious.

GROWING FRUIT

There is a special delight that comes with the growing of fruit – a pleasure that has been felt by gardeners centuries and continents apart. There is still a sense of positive faith in the future involved with planting a fruit tree, and there are few things more satisfying than a basket of ripe dessert gooseberries in ivory, green, gold and red or the bite from the first ripe apple or pear of the season. There is, in addition, the beauty of the spring blossom and the fragrance of apple and plum blossom. In North America, the temperate parts of the southern hemisphere, and on the European mainland, gardeners can also enjoy cherries, but in Britain the birds seem to be particularly avid for this fruit and, unless the trees are caged (which makes the garden look like a zoo), we can enjoy the extravagant blossom but do not expect much fruit.

In your own garden, fruits not readily available commercially can be grown, including quinces and medlars and, in warmer countries, different varieties and species of apricots and peach. Growing for yourself also presents the best chance for tasting fruits at their best – pears, for example, have only a short period of perfect flavour and ripeness. Most fruits are ornamental as well as edible, and grapevines

RIGHT **Part of a potager in soft tones, the greens and blue-greens of the vegetable and salad plants brought out by the little wild heartsease *Viola*. It is not difficult to achieve beauty in the kitchen garden; the colours and textures of the vegetables are so subtle and beautiful, that they lend themselves to patterning and colour composition.**

LEFT A mature pear tree espalier with four tiers. Although a tree like this will need pruning twice a year, it will fruit heavily and also perform the role of a living trellis. This is a French variety, 'Belle Epine du Mas'. It is important to choose a type that takes equally to both restricted growth and hard pruning.

HOW TO MAKE AN ESPALIER

Training an espalier is not difficult; it will be individually tailored and far cheaper than purchasing one. Both apples and pears make good espaliers. Consult your nursery about the variety and rootstock that is best for your purpose and locality, and the size and number of tiers you desire. It is best to have two or three espalier trees, chosen so that good pollination can occur.

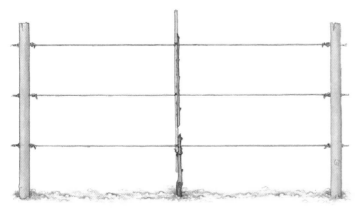

1 *Autumn:* Make scaffolding of end posts and wires (at tier height) to the size you want your mature tree to be. Plant a small 'maiden' fruit tree, keeping the knobbly bit that is the graft above the soil. Cut the top to just above the first wire, making sure there are two buds below.

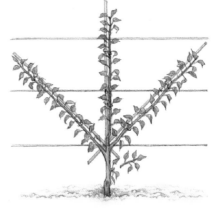

2 *First summer:* Tie the central, leading, shoot vertically to a cane as it develops. Select two strong side branches and tie them to canes that a set at an angle of about 45° to the trunk. *Autumn:* Gradually lower the canes supporting the lateral branches until they are horizontal.

3 *Next winter:* Encourage the second tier by cutting the central leader (trunk) to a bud just above the second wire, ensuring that there are two strong buds below. Prune the horizontal first-tier banches by a third back to a bud that faces outwards.

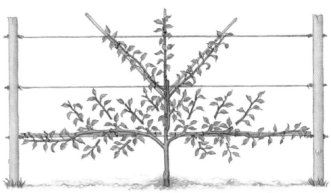

4 *Next summer:* Tie in the new branches of the second tier at 45°, as before. Cut the sideshoot growth on a lower tier to three to four leaves. *Autumn:* Lower the second-tier branches to a horizontal position. Continue tying and pruning until you have the right number of tiers.

RIGHT Ripening medlar fruits. A medlar makes a small, beautiful tree, hardy and easy to grow in a restricted space. It has a lovely, slighty weeping form, thick foliage, rose-like flowers and strange fruits, that can either be eaten ripe with port after a few frosts have softened them or made into a jelly.

BELOW A kitchen garden, integrated into the wider framework of the landscape, and falling to a lake. It is separated by a lowish hedge that allows the blossom of the apple trees to be seen from afar.

and vines of kiwi fruit, and (in warmer climates) passion fruit make a useful as well as beautiful drapery for open-beam pergolas or trellis. On one large wall of St Catherine's College in Oxford there is a strikingly trained ornamental grape 'Brant' – clear green in spring and summer, it turns rich crimson in autumn, with tiny bunches of sweet, dark grapes hanging at neat intervals.

Research into ways of growing fruit have resulted in developments in rootstock that have greatly increased possibilities for better fruit growing. It is of course possible to grow an apple from a pip – unique kinds of fruit tree growing along motorway banks, where people have thrown away pips and cores, testify to this, but the resulting fruit will not be the same as either of the parent trees. It is a real thrill to experiment with pips in this way, but it takes five years or so before the young trees to begin to fruit and we can tell if they will be good or not. Unfortunately, most of us have neither the time nor space to indulge in this procedure, although sometimes this can happen by accident, when a tree from a discarded core grows up in an odd corner.

If you buy a named variety on a recognized rootstock from a reputable nursery, you can have fruit within a year or so and be fairly confident of the flavour and the ultimate size of your tree. With the revival of interest in fruit, you can now buy ready-trained fruit trees, skilfully shaped by an expert. Alternatively, it is possible to train your own tree to the shape you desire: a short trunk with a goblet shape, for example, that could line a kitchen garden area; a living trellis of espalier; or a fan planted against the wall. Some of the shapes are a little extreme for a natural style and rather difficult to maintain, but an espalier is simple to train and the results are fruitful as well as decorative.

For those who prefer a tree with a natural shape, there is still a wide choice. Nearly all fruit trees are grafted, so you can have a dwarf tree to fit a small space, a tree that branches out at about shoulder height (known as half-standard), a large spreading tree (standard), or gradations in between. Quince with its pink blossom and medlar, with its white rose-like flowers, are naturally small trees. There is also variation in size and vigour between cultivars.

OPPOSITE A kitchen garden happily integrated within the leisure garden: herbs and vegetables grow alongside flowers and shrubs, while the flowering fruit trees have bulbs planted around their bases in a wide lawn.

WILDLIFE IN THE GARDEN

BELOW **This dragonfly (*Aeshna cyanea*) prefers to breed in ponds with lots of plants. It is remarkably unafraid of people and does not dart away like many other species of dragonfly. It is a late-season insect, laying its eggs on floating vegetation. The eggs overwinter in a state of suspended animation.**

A garden without movement and sound is inconceivable. The individual voices of birds and the characteristic flight patterns of birds and insects can become as familiar as the personal characteristics of close family and friends. When you are in the garden you learn to sense things on the edges of your consciousness – the swoop of a hawk, the flutter of finches, the bold flight of thrushes, the determined trajectory of dragonflies, the direct beat of some butterflies compared with the delicate flutterings of others. A fleeting glimpse of deer, the sharp tang of fox or tomcat, encounters with lizards and newts – these too are all part of the garden experience.

You do not have to live in a wilderness to appreciate wildlife – wild creatures abound even in the centre of towns and cities. You can find them in the air or the fabric of buildings, in tree trunks, amongst the foliage of climbers and bushes, even underfoot in the soil. One recommendation for sitting quietly in the garden or working half-concealed in a quiet corner is that you can then catch a glimpse of the other life around you.

This is the *alter ego* of the garden, the place animals either regard as home or as a place to visit. Although any garden will attract some creatures, you can purposely plan to make it more welcoming. In practice, gardens managed for a natural style with the appropriate development of different habitats will attract far more creatures than an overgrown wildness that is mistakenly expected to appeal to wild creatures. The more varied kinds of habitat you have and the wider the range of plants you present to the animal world, the better chance you have of attracting a diversity of wildlife. In addition, the presence of many different species in a complex mixed planting means that you are more likely to have a predator population to match those regarded as pests. There are also things you can do in terms of planting and structuring the garden that can make it more of a haven for those creatures you wish to encourage.

Your invitation to the natural world will almost always be answered. Provide some water in the garden or set up a feeding station for birds and the response will be immediate. Build a nature-friendly wall or create a patch of permanent grassland and things will eventually begin to happen. Some animals attracted to the garden will take up residency, while others – such as migratory birds and butterflies or creatures seeking solace from unfriendly weather – will come as seasonal or occasional visitors.

The more your awareness grows of the complex web of life forms supported within even a quite conventional garden, the more understanding you develop. This in turn leads to a more intelligent and sympathetic way of managing a garden.

OPPOSITE **Very beautiful butterflies of the colourful family Nymphalidae: the small tortoiseshell (*Aglais urticae*) and the peacock (*Inachis io*) sipping nectar from *Inula hookeri*. Both species of butterfly lay their eggs on nettles, the tortoiseshell preferring young tender plants, the peacock larger and more vigorous plants.**

WILDLIFE ATTRACTED TO GARDENS

The eighteenth century saw an extraordinary renaissance in science, rational thought and the observation of natural history. Although people explored far and wide, sending back observations and opinions, another quieter achievement in the study of natural history was just as important and far reaching. The naturalist parson, Gilbert White (1720–93) saw that travelling abroad was not the only means of education, but that careful observations in one place could yield new and important knowledge. His own quiet but incredibly thorough observations in his garden and its immediate environs brought several new insights to natural science and set a model that is still valid.

Garden naturalists can make their contribution. One contemporary British gardener, Dr Jennifer Owen, observed the plants and animals in her garden over a period of fifteen years and found, when she summarized her findings, that a quite extraordinary number of birds, plants, spiders and invertebrates lived alongside her. Even more startling, was the fact that this ecological study was carried out not in a rural idyll but in a medium-sized garden in the suburb of an industrial city in the English Midlands – with a lawn, flowerbeds, rockery, neat paths and mixed plantings of flowers, vegetables and salad greens. The entire plot is a typical townhouse shape, a long rectangle of about 741 sq m (886 sq yd), of which slightly over a third is taken up by the house, garage and garage forecourt. Yet in this small compass there are several hundred different kinds of plant, 21 kinds of butterflies, 68 species of moth, and representatives of many other animal groups, such as bees, ants, woodlice, spiders and birds. I was pleased to notice four different kinds of hoverfly in my more southerly garden, but this is nothing beside Dr Owen's keen discerning observations. She identified hundreds of individuals and a total of 91 species in her garden in

BELOW **A vista of mounded** *Sedum spectabile*, **a perennial species that people as well as birds and insects find attractive. Clipped box grows in the foreground with yellow** *Anthemis* **'E.C. Buxton' flourishing behind it.**

Leicestershire. There is a similar number of plants and creatures in almost all gardens – it is simply a matter of seeing them, and of developing the food plants and an increased diversity of habitat that can sustain them.

Other studies have shown a remarkable diversity of wildlife in urban gardens. It is now known that large cities such as London have their own microclimate. Under conditions that may be a degree warmer than the nearest countryside, wild flora and fauna thrive and gardeners can confidently grow warmer-climate species that their rural counterparts would not dare attempt, thus providing an extra band of plants for wildlife to colonize. Mammals are also visitors to some gardens. Foxes and badgers come to European gardens and raccoons to North American ones. It is not unusual for hummingbirds to come in to feed on nectar-rich shrubs and trees in city gardens in California, and birds such as bulbuls, wax finches, blue jays, chickadees and cardinals frequent gardens in many places in North America. In Britain, farmland birds, such as linnets and bullfinches, are nesting in gardens as the agricultural landscape becomes increasingly less habitable.

It used to be said that native species of plant were always superior to introductions and exotics in terms of the abundance of wildlife they can support.

ABOVE **A pleasant scene in a New York community garden, with an ideal plant mixture where flowers, fruits, salad greens and vegetables nudge along side by side. Community gardens (official and unofficial), especially those within large towns, have beneficial effects for both their human and animal residents.**

LEFT **A common and widespread New World species, the American robin (*Turdus migratorius*) is a frequent visitor to urban gardens. Besides berries, it also eats worms and insects, nesting in shrubs and trees, on sheltered windowsills and under the eaves of houses.**

Subsequent research has shown a more complex pattern, with many garden introductions and naturalized plants scoring very high for wildlife benefit. Introduced conifers present shelter for small birds and invertebrates in places where large native evergreens are either rare or lacking. Many garden flowers are extremely rich in nectar and in many gardens non-natives provide early and late blooms that are vital to end-of-season insects.

Native plants are especially important where they form part of a complex cycle of nutrition and breeding, such as that of the blue butterflies (Lycaenidae). Studies that were carried out because of the extinction of the large blue (*Maculinea arion*) in Britain in 1979 found that the cycle involves fine-grazed turf growing in the right aspect, special food plants and ants (of the genus *Myrmica*) that look after the butterfly chrysalis and larva. A similar cycle is believed to apply (with specific adaptations) to many of the butterflies in this large family (including the hairstreak and argus groups). Nearly all butterflies have particular grasses or plant groups that are absolutely necessary to their survival.

The lives of insects are a small marvel of unbelievable complexity and to replicate precise conditions in order to entice a rarity into the garden would be very difficult. Starting from the opposite position, and growing plants that are known to attract butterflies, especially the favourites of those species you have actually seen in the garden, may well help the survival of local populations. It is also useful to provide places where butterflies can overwinter.

OPPOSITE **Three late-season garden bumble bees, of the commonest garden species (*Bombus hortorum*), explore the florets of the beautiful eryngium known as Miss Willmott's ghost (*Eryngium giganteum*). This eryngium provides a welcome supply of late nectar for insects.**

FLOWERS THAT ATTRACT BIRDS, AND BUTTERFLIES, BEES, HOVERFLIES AND OTHER INSECTS

Aster novae-anglia, A. novi-belgii, etc. **Michaelmas daisy**
> butterflies, moths and other late-feeding insects

Aubretia **aubretia**
> attracts butterflies that have hibernated as adults and other flying insects

Buddleja davidii **buddleja**
> butterflies, moths, hummingbird hawkmoths and other insects

Crataegus **hawthorns**
> provides shelter and berries for birds; nectar, pollen and foliage for moths and butterflies

Echinacea **cone flower**
> flowers attract bees and butterflies

Hedera helix **ivy**
> late flowers for butterflies, bees, moths; berries for birds; provides shelter

Humulus **hop**
> food for butterfly larvae; shelter for birds and insects

Iberis **candytuft**
> bees, early-flying butterflies and moths, and beetles

Lavandula **lavender**
> flowers attract bees, butterflies and other insects

Lonicera **honeysuckle**
> nectar-rich flowers attract bees, butterflies and hummingbirds

Lunaria annua **honesty**
> annual that feeds butterfly larvae and adults; birds eat seeds

Malus domestica **apple**
> blossom attracts bees; fruit food for birds and butterflies

Melissa officialis **lemon balm, bee balm**
> flowers attract butterflies; ripe spikes attract seed-eating birds

Monarda didyma **bergamot, bee balm**
> midsummer flowers attract bees and hummingbirds

Rudbeckia **rudbeckia**
> flowers attract bees and butterflies

Rudbeckia hirta **black-eyed Susan**
> butterflies, bees, hoverflies and many other insects

Salvia **sages**
> bees, butterflies, hummingbirds love flowers of different species

Sedum spectabile **stonecrop**
> bees, butterflies and almost all late-flying insects

Thymus **thyme**
> butterflies, bees, hoverflies and many other insects

Tilia **lime tree**
> bunches of sweet nectar in spring attracts bees and moths

Urtica **stinging nettle**
> if grown in a sunny place, butterfly larvae feed on food plant

Verbascum **verbascum**
> flowers attract bees; foliage food for moths

Different species tackle the period of winter cold in different ways. The brightly coloured, active small copper (*Lycaena phlaeas*), a frequent visitor to gardens, is unusual in that it hibernates as a caterpillar on the young leaves of sorrel plants (*Rumex acetosa* and *R. acetosella*). The white butterflies (family Pieridae) hibernate in chrysalis form, typically attached to a stem by a silken girdle. This group, which also includes the charming orange-tip butterfly (*Anthocharis cardamines*) and the large and small whites (*Pieris brassicae* and *P. rapae*) which, once scarce, grew common with the increase in farming, feeds on cultivated plants such as cabbages and turnips. The small white spread from its native Eurasia to colonize North America in the early nineteenth century and Australia in the twentieth century. In gardens, even vegetable gardens, they are very rarely serious pests, particularly if there is a mixed economy of plants and the gardener keeps a wary eye for the eggs and small larvae that feed on the undersides of leaves.

The monarch butterfly hibernates as an adult in fir forests. It has also colonized places where its main food plant – milkweed – has been introduced into warm-climate gardens, as in the Canary Islands, the Azores and Australasia. *Asclepias tuberosa* is actually known as butterfly weed, although it is also attractive to bees. Another migratory butterfly, the beautiful painted lady (*Cynthia cardui*) – also known as the cosmopolitan butterfly in the USA – is frequently seen in gardens and is thought to overwinter as a chrysalis on the edges of deserts. Although neither as big nor as strong a flyer as the monarch, it can traverse oceans and continents, and has been seen up to 3,000 km (2,000 miles) from its winter breeding grounds. It roams widely, feeding on a variety of flowers, including scabiouses and thistles. Several generations of this short-lived species may breed during a good summer, with eggs typically laid on thistles, although they also sometimes choose nettles and mallows.

OPPOSITE **A path mown through a sea of flowering Yorkshire fog (*Holcus mollis*) in an orchard. Permanent grass is a prime habitat for butterflies and small mammals.**

RIGHT **A monarch butterfly (*Danaus plexippus*), the largest and most spectacular of migratory butterflies, feeds on the florets of *Lysimachia clethroides*. The caterpillar feeds mainly on milkweeds, from which it derive toxins, which inhibit most other creatures from eating it.**

BIRDS AND BATS IN THE GARDEN

Gardens are special places to us, but they also represent a sizeable portion of land. In Britain, it has been estimated that gardens occupy 1.2 million acres (5 million ha) of land (more than the total for nature reserves), and their importance to wildlife is increasing as mechanized agri-business makes farmland less accommodating. Gardens are unusual, compared with other small patches of land, in that they contain a greater number of different habitats within a small space. This is all the more true of a garden where a natural style has been adopted.

We look out on our gardens each day and think we see them but there is far more than meets the eye stirring among the branches, beneath the leaves and below the soil. It is remarkable to think that, despite close acquaintance over millennia, there is still so much we do not yet know even about the wildlife that lives closest to us. A consequence of this is that any one of us with a keen eye and clear perception can make an observation that is new to science. To take one example, house martins have been making their nests on the sides of buildings for centuries and feeding in the gardens round about. Yet it was only comparatively recently established that house-martin siblings help the parents to bring up second broods so that they are all well fed and fit for migration at the end of the summer.

Many people nowadays put food out for birds, and the bird population has come to rely on this supplementary source of nutrition. It also gives garden-owners the pleasure of being able to watch a considerable range of birds, that also feed on

ABOVE The house martin (*Delichon urbica*) originally nested on cliffs in wild countryside, but it took readily to human constructions, such as bridges, and to houses, where it now make its cup-shaped nest under the eaves. House martins may raise several broods in a season.

LEFT Blackbirds (*Turdus merula*) are one of the few bird species that has not suffered the disastrous decline in numbers suffered by most British birds, possibly because they are omnivorous and can find food in both urban and country gardens in the form of insects and berries. Hawthorn (*in the picture*) is a good source of food.

A LAWN BIRD-FEEDER

ABOVE An all-purpose bird table, mounted in a lawn on a stake. The height above ground should prevent cats from leaping up but the metal collar adds an extra barrier and also deters squirrels. The gaps on the tray allow water to drain away after downpours of rain.

A HANGING BIRD-FEEDER

ABOVE This bird-feeding tray is designed to hang from a branch (or from a wall bracket). It is a better deterrent to cats than a mounted table, although squirrels will have no difficulty in reaching it. Make sure you do not leave stale food on feeders, as this can cause disease.

ABOVE Bird feeders with squirrel baffles usually (but not always) prevent these crafty rodents from stealing nuts intended for garden birds.

LEFT Hummingbirds frequent gardens in the USA that have nectar-rich, brightly-coloured flowers, especially those that are trumpet-shaped. The ruby-throated hummingbird is the most widespread (from southern Canada to the the Gulf of Mexico) and common in gardens; the black-throated hummingbird may be seen sometimes on garden plants, but is westerly in distribution.

HOW TO MAKE A NEST BOX

Bird-conservation organizations have designs for nest boxes suitable for different species of bird. Some have entry holes in the front (used by tits, sparrows or starlings, depending on size); some are open-fronted (for use by robins, wrens and (if larger) kestrels). A few species prefer side entrances, and hole-nesting owls will sometimes use a long open-topped box, known as a 'chimney box'.

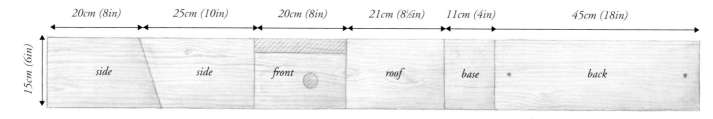

1 This standard nest box can be made easily and inexpensively, out of a plank of timber, following a simple cutting plan (*see above*). The pieces are screwed together and an adjustable bit used to drill out the entry/exit hole, the size varying depending on the bird species you wish to attract. The perch can be omitted as it may encourage predators.

2 The entry hole in the front should be no more than 29mm (1⅛in) for great tits and blue tits. If it is larger, sparrows and starlings will also will be able to use it, and are likely to drive away the tits. Woodpeckers may also enlarge the entrance for their own use; spotted flycatchers sometimes use mud to reduce the hole size.

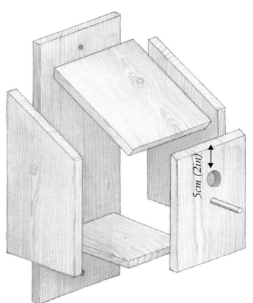

3 Hinge the lid with a piece of webbing or tyre inner tube. The lid is secured with a galvanized (rust-proof) hook and eye. It is is better not to peek inside while there are eggs or young.

LEFT Great tit (*Parus major*) feeding its young in a nest box. This brood of four is relatively small (5–12 eggs is normal). Great tits and blue tits (*Parus caeruleus*) are among the most common users of nest boxes.

garden pests as well as the nuts and birdtable food. Water is vital to bird life, too, but unfortunately fewer garden-owners recognize this need and erect a bird bath. All gardens are visited by wildlife in some shape or form, but most would probably benefit from an environmental audit that evaluates the existing situation and explores further possibilities. This can be carried out by working your way systematically around the garden, trying to see how it looks from a wildlife perspective.

A nicely kept lawn with grasses and rosette-leaved wildflowers will be used by a range of animals. Ants, spiders and beetles will run over the surface; bees, moth caterpillars and other insects will feed there; and there will be an even greater number of creatures in the litter layer and in the soil below. This activity attracts ground-feeding birds, and it has been shown that suburban birds use lawns far more than they do comparable areas of arable or natural grassland. Birds that are familiar vistors to European garden lawns include wagtails, sparrows, dunnocks, thrushes, starlings, blackbirds, and migrant fieldfares and redwings, as well as pigeons and collared doves. Because blackbirds are omnivorous, they also take advantage of bird tables and fruiting hedges and trees. The blackbird population of gardens in England has been estimated at twenty times that of the surrounding countryside. In North American cities the American robin is also extremely common, especially in urban gardens. It must be remembered, however, that the groundsman's 'perfect' garden lawn is very heavy on resources as well as pesticides. Less formal lawns that are kept at 3–5cm (1–2in) can thrive without artificial feeding (and be cut where appropriate by a mulch-mower); if wildflowers are allowed, these lawns make better sense and are more appealing to wildlife. In dry, hot climates it might be better to consider a lawn alternative such as a heather bed around a flagstone terrace or a collection of ornamental grasses.

ABOVE **Nest boxes should be placed where predators will have trouble reaching them. The design and height above ground of the box should be appropriate for the species you are trying to attract. This box, situated in an oak tree, would suit a sparrow or, if the entrance hole were small, great tits and blue tits.**

Longer grass provides shelter for small mammals and larger insects, such as grasshoppers and crickets. The larvae of butterflies, moths and many other insects can overwinter on grasses and other wild plants. Some butterfly species are conservative about where they lay their eggs, and a large garden that has an area set aside as long grass (an orchard, for example) can be of significant conservation value. It is better to let grass grow naturally in an orchard, since fruit trees suffer from competition with close-mown grass. The seedheads of grassland plants are also an important food source. Ants' nests in longer grass provide an extra incentive for woodpeckers to visit the garden.

Birds, especially finches, also appreciate garden plants that produce large seedheads. The affinity of finches for the thistle family (including many garden-worthy ones) is well known; they also love sunflowers. Yarrow (*Achillea millifolia*), globe thistle (*Echinops ritro*), golden rod (*Solidago canadensis*), rose campion (*Lychnis coronaria*), chicory (*Cichorium intybus*) and snapdragon (*Antirrhinum*) are all plants that produce attractive flowers and good seed. Birds are the most visible seed-eaters, but other animals, such as ants and beetles, appreciate them as well, taking the seeds away as soon as they have fallen. Indeed ants are responsible for sowing and spreading a number of plant species.

Trees give shelter, nesting places and food for birds. Insects and other invertebrates live in crevices in the bark and insectivorous birds will feed on them. In open places, trunk and branches are also colonized by lichens which will provide food for a microfauna and do the trees no harm at all. Flowering trees and shrubs give nectar for birds and insects, and berries and other fruits from late summer through to the winter. Buddleja, which has spread to naturalize in many places throughout the world, is a marvellously rich source of nectar and seed, attracting an incredible diversity of butterflies, moths, bees, wasps, lacewings and other insects. Extra nesting places can be provided by putting up nest boxes, although care has to be taken over siting, since many predators can also climb or fly.

Hedges and coniferous trees with dense foliage give shelter and nest sites to birds and are particularly significant for small birds who have difficulty in keeping warm during hard winters. Butterflies may also roost in hedges, although walls draped by climbers are even more useful. Some birds may also nest in holes and crevices of walls that are covered by foliage, notably wrens and robins in the lower reaches and flycatchers at higher levels. Climbing plants can be a great boon for wildlife as well as a joy to gardeners. A vast diversity of invertebrate life also thrives in the damp shade on and within walls, including woodlice, spiders, beetles and ants. Nest boxes placed on walls are generally safer for the inhabitants than those in trees, although they should not be sited in direct sun.

Finally, you should not forget the soil itself. In an organically rich garden soil, huge numbers of tiny and microscopic creatures are actively busy. We are familiar with the larger ones, such as earthworms, slugs, snails, centipedes, millipedes, spiders, woodlice, springtails, ants and beetles, but while we know the names of most of our garden birds, there are few gardeners who can distinguish one woodlouse from another or have any idea of the identity of the thousands of different beetles. The microorganisms exist in countless billions, decomposing and recycling the organic matter in the soil. One group in particular is responsible for the sweet fresh smell of good soil and well-made compost. Attempting to single out friend and foe amongst all these is a largely unrewarding – it is preferable to add compost and other humus-rich material and to grow a mixture of plants that thrive in their selected positions in order to promote a natural balance.

BELOW **This open-fronted box is stuffed with hollow plant stems. Tucked away within the ivy, they present a sheltered site, where overwintering insects can shelter comfortably. The scheme is evidently a success as this box has at least five occupants.**

HOW TO MAKE A BAT BOX

Bat boxes are not quite so successful with their intended residents as garden-bird boxes, but it is well worth the effort of putting a few in place, because bats are such delightful creatures. Bats suffer from lack of habitat, so bat boxes in suitable gardens can be very valuable. Because most bats move roosts fairly frequently, your box may not be occupied full time, but do not open it through curiosity.

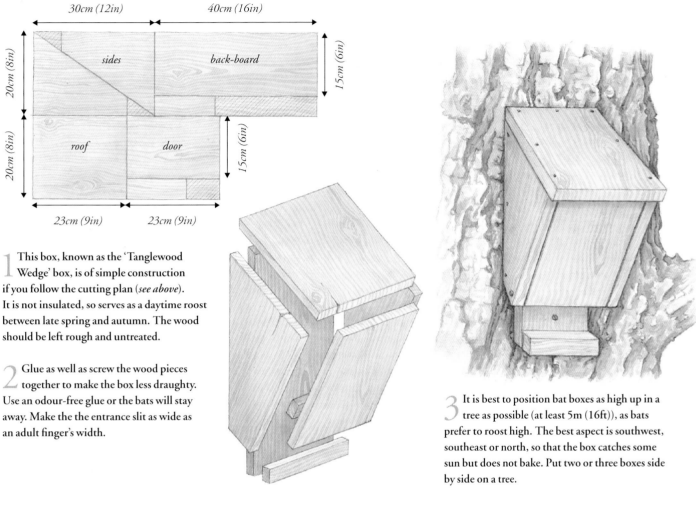

1 This box, known as the 'Tanglewood Wedge' box, is of simple construction if you follow the cutting plan (*see above*). It is not insulated, so serves as a daytime roost between late spring and autumn. The wood should be left rough and untreated.

2 Glue as well as screw the wood pieces together to make the box less draughty. Use an odour-free glue or the bats will stay away. Make the the entrance slit as wide as an adult finger's width.

3 It is best to position bat boxes as high up in a tree as possible (at least 5m (16ft)), as bats prefer to roost high. The best aspect is southwest, southeast or north, so that the box catches some sun but does not bake. Put two or three boxes side by side on a tree.

LEFT Bat boxes should not be too exposed, but the flight path to them should be unimpeded. The wood will weather so the boxes will quickly become part of the scenery. If there is no sign of occupancy (such as droppings on the batten step or through direct observation) after a year or so, move the box to another site.

LEISURE IN THE GARDEN

There is something special about eating out of doors, particularly in the easy informality that a natural style confers upon a garden. A table with chairs for all the family, and a friend or two, can be a semi-permanent fixture beneath a tree or by a pool, making it easy for regular eating out *en famille*. A bench in a sunny place by the back door provides a place to open mail or to prepare vegetables. There is also a need for occasional chairs, benches and cushions that can be taken into the private shade, either for quiet contemplation on your own or for teenagers to find a secluded spot to hide away.

A garden in which the plants have a certain autonomy is forever changing and will always be interesting. There is invariably a plant coming into flower, or something that is so stunningly at its peak that it stops you in your tracks. Birds or other animals attract the attention of anyone with a few moments to spare. There is also the pleasure of cutting flowers and composing posies and bouquets for the house, and of picking fruits and vegetables, as well as the practical joy of gardening itself. The pure refreshment of wandering outside, even if just for a few moments, and letting your attention wander and soaking in the atmosphere is a simple tonic that should not be overlooked.

Gardens mean a great deal to children, although one should not expect them to show their feelings in obvious ways. They rarely show any marked desire to hoe or weed (but then how many adults really enjoy the repetitive chores of gardening). For children, their gardens are secret places, where they can investigate the scents and sounds, taking in their impressions, so that later in life, the perfume of a particular rose, the tang of privet flower or a bird's song will transport them back to childhood.

While it is important to provide play places for children, it is equally if not more important to allow them to find their own way around the garden. They may like to sleep in the long grass, make daisy chains on the lawn, hide in arbours, make castles of large fallen trunks or climb trees (there are few more enjoyable pastimes than sitting hidden in the branches of a tree, with an apple and a favourite cat). Some children like to grow things, but often this is something that comes with age, and to try to force the pace can put them off. Most children, however, like eating, and to give a child a strawberry patch, or a plum or apple tree, or a fruit bush that is their very own, and from which they can pick their own fruit, can be the start of a lifelong affinity both for the garden and for healthy eating.

LEFT **A small bed with something delicious in it, such as strawberries, may draw a child to enjoy the garden much better than a purely decorative bed. They can eat the strawberries as they ripen or gather them in a bowl to share with the rest of the family.**

OPPOSITE **A tree house is a dream for almost every child – and indeed for many adults. This house is sturdy, high and brand new. As it ages, it will weather to the shade of the ash tree in which it is lodged. When making a tree house, it is important to make sure the ladder is safe and securely fixed.**

PLAY IN THE GARDEN

Play in the garden is not confined to the younger age group. Swings should be strong enough to support an adult (a Watteau fantasy is open to anyone), and a large seesaw is as inviting to grown-ups as to children. Secure a long-planked seesaw between two heavy metal wheels and you can move it to prevent wear being concentrated in one place.

Swings are lovely things to have in a garden and, apart from their obvious pleasures, help children to develop a good sense of balance. The simplest, and often the most enjoyed kind, can be made by hanging a car tyre securely from a strong branch of a tree. It makes for good fun if the children can then swing over a stream or ditch. A straightforward flat-platform swing can also be hung from a tree, but if

you have no trees suitable or large enough, most shops sell them with free-standing supports. To be safe, the supports must be firmly secured, preferably sunk in a concrete base. A thick layer of chipped bark beneath makes for a soft landing and saves the mess and mud that occurs when the grass wears thin.

If you live in the country or have friends with access to tree trunks, consider importing some trunks to your garden. Having their own rustic seat in a quiet place or a 'tree trunk throne' appeals to most children. I have known many instances where a child has consistently preferred to play and climb over tree-trunks than to use commercial play equipment or a Wendy house. Perhaps the most exciting event is when a really big tree comes down

ABOVE A rough-hewn, two-seater throne seat, with a luxuriant canopy of common ivy (*Hedera helix*). A floral element is supplied by the hardy geraniums and sedum growing on either side.

LEFT Swings need to be securely secured, but the structure can be something of an eye-sore. Here, the structural poles are swathed with climbing roses. Adults will go on enjoying this particular swing after the children have grown up or just allow it to be used as a trellis for the roses.

HOW TO MAKE GARDEN FURNITURE

Tree trunks from your own or your friends' felled trees can be used to make garden furniture that fits suitably into a natural-style garden. The trunks will have to be sound and fairly large. You will need only a chain-saw to make the furniture, but if you are not used to using one of these machines, it is wiser to find someone with experience who could do it for you.

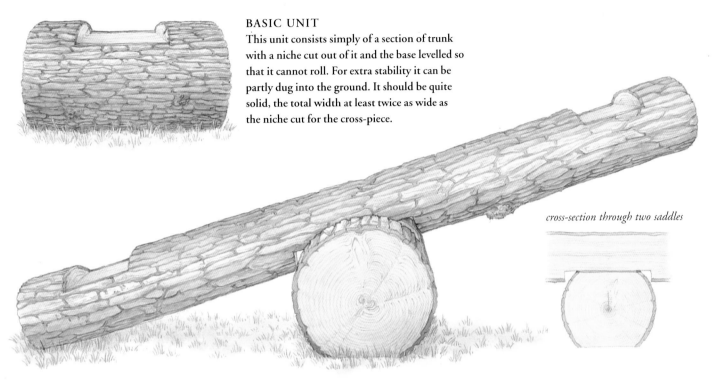

BASIC UNIT

This unit consists simply of a section of trunk with a niche cut out of it and the base levelled so that it cannot roll. For extra stability it can be partly dug into the ground. It should be quite solid, the total width at least twice as wide as the niche cut for the cross-piece.

cross-section through two saddles

SEESAW

This seesaw consists of a basic unit, used as a base. Instead of a normal plank, you can use a tree trunk with niche seats cut at either end on the surface that will be the upper part of the seesaw. Cut a saddle underneath in the centre of the lower surface. This should fit fairly snugly into the saddle in the basic unit, to prevent the seesaw from shifting or swaying.

THRONE SEAT

This rustic chair could not be simpler. Cut an L-shape from a log, making the seat higher or lower, depending on whom it is intended for. In uneven ground, dig the seat in to secure it.

BENCH

The rustic bench calls for two basic units and a log cut in two down the centre, with two saddles that slot into those of the basic units. If you have two logs to work with, you can make two matching benches, using one log for the four basic units; the other log divided in two makes the two flat-topped seats. This style of rustic furniture will weather with the years, but even when made out of poor-quality timber it should last for a long while.

and youngsters can swarm all over it, climbing, riding and sailing it, until the bark comes off and the inner wood turns ivory. They will be grown up before it decays completely.

There is, of course, a great deal of difference between the desires of toddlers, teenage children and adults, let alone the different needs of all the individuals involved. No hope then of pleasing everybody, but if one can generalize, it is true to say that children have a kind of recognition of good places, just as wild creatures do. Create a garden that has a natural flow in which the plants and wildlife thrive and there is a pretty good chance that all age-groups will find a niche which will match their moods and needs. It is up to you to maintain the diversity, then leave it to them to choose.

Larger gardens can afford space for a tennis court, and even these inherently ugly structures can be integrated into the overall style by planting half-standard fruit trees around the periphery, so that the tracery of branches, blossom and leaves, disguises the chain link surrounds. A basketball net takes up so little room, it could be fitted into almost any garden. If space is at a premium, a spring meadow can be rough-mown a few weeks after flowering, to provide a turf pitch for ball games for children during the summer and autumn.

Most serious gardeners keep a garden book that covers the plain details of the garden and its plants. A garden that aspires to a natural style will have more unusual and unexpected changes and progressions than a conventional plot, and making a note of developments, such as plant, animal (and human) visitors, can make an absorbing record. Observations of birds and other animals and *objets trouvés* can also find their way into this record, which can include sketches, plans and collages. Children acting 'nature detective' find a wide range of garden wildlife that you never guessed existed.

A natural garden should attract a wide range of bird life, and observations of unusual species or regular census observations can be of great help to bird-conservation organizations. If your observations are more casual and sporadic, make an aide-mémoire with a garden-bird chart, and mark off those that have come into the garden. Use different marks for birds seen flying over the garden, including passing migrants, birds that have actually come into the garden, and birds that have bred in the garden. Parents who start this as a project for their children often end up continuing after their offspring have grown up and left home. Children find a pleasure in learning how to observe and identify birds that may last them for the rest of their lives.

BELOW A dwarf apple tree heavily laden with fruit. The dwarfing rootstock limits growth to manageable proportions for a small garden. The apple is the familiar 'Golden Delicious' which, when grown in good organic soil and picked at the right moment, does actually live up to its name.

The living world has an extraordinary complexity, even in a fairly new small garden which would be described by its owners as simple and perfectly ordinary. The natural world penetrates every corner and can be seen as a kind of living museum.

SEASONAL OBSERVATIONS

The Chinese have a game called 'looking for spring' in which they search for the first signs of reawakening life. These might include a bird breaking into song or the first buds appearing after winter, the first break of blossom or agitation among winter migrant birds. It is a cheerful game and can be carried out anywhere.

Summer is a good time for doing bird observations, a garden census for example, or a detailed study of one nest box. It has been estimated that blue-tit parents need to find something like 15,000 caterpillars in order to raise a single brood. Other members of the tit and chickadee group have similar requirements. That amount of caterpillars represents many trips to and from the nest. When do the parents start? Do they get the food nearby?

Count the trips they make in five minutes? If you watch carefully and are lucky, you may see the baby birds coming out to fly for the first time.

Autumn is usually a good period for observing spiders. How many different kinds inhabit the garden? Do they all have webs? What is the geometry of an orb web? Do spiders fly? Try bringing a trowel-full of leaf litter indoors. Put it on a tray and look through a hand lens or magnifying glass, as after a few minutes it comes to life. On a conservative estimate, it could contain earthworms and slugs, millepedes, insects and insect larvae, woodlice and spiders. A microscope would discover quantities of microfauna, microfungi and millions of bacteria. All these are necessary to complete the process of recycling the leaves and other dead and dying organic matter.

If winter brings snow, tracks are intriguing. You may find animals in the garden you never guessed were there. Look for cones and nuts: you can tell what has been eating them by the pattern of bites, nibbles or beak blows. There is also the puzzle of where insects go in winter. The complete life cycle of

ABOVE **You need to have a large garden with some water if you want to keep ducks, but they are most friendly and rewarding creatures. This motley little domestic flock includes Aylesbury ducks, hybrid mallards, tufted ducks and mandarin. It is essential to shut them up in a secure hutch at night or they may be eaten by foxes.**

even quite familiar garden insects is not fully known or understood, but the birds know where to find them. You can see birds working their way along branches (sometimes while they are awaiting their turn at the nut-feeder) and down the rough bark of trunks, as well as in crevices in walls, where they can find concealed insects and bugs.

FOUND OBJECTS IN THE GARDEN

I am always surprised by the sheer number of things of interest to be discovered in a garden. Items that are dug up while the ground is being cultivated are one distinct area in which older gardens can yield a trail of history. Among the objects found by our family and friends are fossils, carved flints, clay pipe stems and bowls, antique bottles and pots. More numerous are pieces of crockery, rusted old knives and kitchen implements. The shape, quality and patterning of the pottery can be interesting, but rusted metal should be treated with caution. A local history society or museum may be able to help with the dating and identification of many of the objects. The most interesting items can be assembled and labelled and made into an extemporary garden museum. You may want to keep some of them

BELOW **Autumn is the time for spiders' webs. The dew and sunlight catch the beauty of an orb spider's web and several woolly hammocks made by funnel spiders. The webs are slung on the twigs of berberis and roses, but spiders are not choosy; any dense shrub will suit them.**

permanently. On the other hand, children sometimes become fascinated with items that are of no interest to grown-ups. Stones, pebbles and flints rate high in this category, especially among younger children, and there is no reason why these too, should not be part of the garden museum exhibition.

PETS

As they get older many children yearn for pets. The foremost principles here should be that an animal is an individual in its own right and not an animated cuddly toy, and that all animals need appropriate attention and places to live. Animal-welfare organizations will advise on the needs and care of pet animals. Some animals, especially those used to living alongside humans, such as cats and dogs, do not fret at close contact with people, and these make the most rewarding pets. For many years our family enjoyed keeping ducks, and as far as we could tell the ducks liked us, but you need to be able to provide water and a separate pen or the run of an orchard since ducks are no respecters of plant life. There is a domestic breed called Khaki Campbell that is very tame and easily domesticated. They are regular layers, but seem to lack an instinct for brooding so do not seem to mind when you gather up the eggs. It is, however, essential to shut them up in a secure box at dusk because foxes and other predators are quick to take advantage of animals whose natural defences and sense of fear have been bred out of them.

GARDEN SAFETY

A disturbing level of accidents seems to happen in gardens. Some are inevitable. Who has not worked on into the dusk to get a job finished, when it is too dark by any sensible standards to see clearly, and certainly dangerous to be using sharp tools and power machinery? There are occasions, too, when one has checked just in time an impulse to sort out an exasperating fault in machinery before the blades have stopped moving – many gardeners have lost fingers and toes this way. There are jobs, you think you can just fit into a small amount of time, and then goggles or boots go missing, and there is considerable temptation simply to get on with the task rather than spend a quarter of an hour looking for the missing item.

It is easy to be lazy about safety but wise gardeners will use iron self-discipline to train themselves into the habit of mind that resembles that of a trained horticultural worker. One of the problems for the garden-owner, is that there is a multiplicity of jobs, demanding different skills, none of which you probably do frequently enough to achieve a real level of skill and competence.

In some cases, you do not recognize danger until after the event. I have partially-toed friends who mowed uneven ground in soft shoes, using a rotary mower that spun out of control. I have come across adults, and one sad case of a child, who suffered terribly from skin blistering equivalent to second- and third-degree burns after cutting back undergrowth that included the umbellifers, principally the giant hogweed (*Heracleum mantegazzianum*), but also hogweed (*H. spondylium*) itself. Shorts and thong sandals are utterly inappropriate for tasks such as these. Even everyday plants, such as rose, brambles, blackthorn and pyracantha, can inflict unpleasant gashes and wounds on the unwary. It is necessary to remember that maintenance means clearing or pruning, damaging, uprooting, chopping back or even killing these plants. Plants cannot run away, so they have other means of defending themselves, and it is foolish not to recognize this and clothe yourself accordingly. If you have planned your garden well such jobs should

ABOVE **An outdoor display of shells, in this case marine species. Similar displays could be made with fossils, pieces of clay pipe and other historic artefacts, or with differently sized and coloured snail shells.**

LEFT **An ingenious basket sculpture that can be refilled with different collections of pine cones, leaves, shells, twigs or pebbles arranged in varying patterns. It could also be moved physically to a different part of the garden to make a change, or to mark different seasons.**

ABOVE **This fine collection of old wooden tools is almost a horticultural museum exhibit, but they are all still used. You can buy modern tools that are equally attractive and useful. The multinational nature of contemporary trade also means that we can sample interesting and valuable tools from other countries.**

garden to the places where their children are likely to play. This is a good idea as long as the children conform to expectations, but many of the problems occur when they do not. One thing that is emphasized less than it could be in regard to child safety is to warn them properly. Clearly, with some children this represents a challenge, but if warnings are heeded, being able to recognize and avoid a danger (such as poisonous plants) is better than having the danger lifted out of the way. In the end, the safest thing is to be with the children as much as possible in the garden, and to reinforce the safety requirements when an appropriate situation arises.

Of course, there are precautions that should always be taken, for yourselves as well as for children. Electrically powered tools, for example, should always be plugged into a circuit-breaker. Some countries have a standard requirement for a centrally located circuit-breaker on the main fuse box, but where this is absent, the circuit-breaker must go directly into the mains socket (even when an extension lead is used). Long extension leads are a hazard, particularly in long gardens and when small children are about, since there may be as much as 25m (82ft) of cable that is out of sight. Small petrol- and battery-powered appliances may be preferable in these circumstances. The technology of battery-powered hedge trimmers is developing fast, and these are now quite light and efficient, as well as easier to use. Goggles are an absolute essential in this task, even when the amount of growth is light. It is so easy for a chip of wood, a piece of dirt or a twig to fly up and get into the eye. Using a shredder also demands eye and hearing protection at all times.

be minimized. It is better, for example, to plant a shrub that will grow to fit a space than to put in some large and vigorous plant that forces you into doing battle with it several times a year.

MINIMIZING RISK

Even a garden which aspires to a natural style will need a certain amount of maintenance and it is sensible to accord your plants the courtesy of respect. Minimizing the risk is to do with assessment and regulation of the danger at early stages. Some designs – slippery steps, for example – are inherently dangerous. You may decide to keep them for aesthetic or other reasons, but you need to be aware on your own behalf and to warn others. Some parents like to have a direct sightline right along the

ERGONOMIC TOOLS

It is a good idea to assemble a group of tools that feel good in your hands and that you can operate comfortably and efficiently. This applies to hand tools as much as to powered ones. It is stupid to be straining to dig out a plant with a fork, and levering your back into all kinds of disadvantageous positions, when you would do better using a garden mattock which has more leverage for less power. Nowadays there is a wide range of well-made tools available, some of them borrowed from other countries and cultures. It may well be that, because of your size and build, you would be better off with a long-handled Italian spade or a Vietnamese hoe than the standard designs prevalent in northern Europe or North America.

HOW TO MAKE A PEBBLE POOL

A ground-level pebble pool is safe for children because there is no standing water. The water from the fountain drains through the pebbles into the reservoir below. The layer of pebbles rests on a piece of robust wire mesh, which is supported by a 8cm (3in) ledge.

This is also a good design for introducing water into a small garden, as the pool can take up space as little as 60cm (24in) in diameter. Wind and evaporation cause some water loss but, apart from topping up the reservoir regularly, this design needs little maintenance.

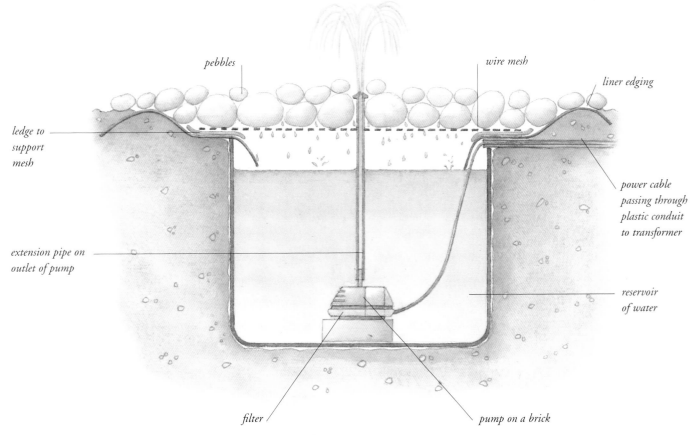

pebbles

wire mesh

liner edging

ledge to support mesh

power cable passing through plastic conduit to transformer

extension pipe on outlet of pump

reservoir of water

filter

pump on a brick

LEFT This pebble-lined pool is different from the illustration above, in that it has a depth, which means it would be unsafe for children. It is made by covering a standard pool with a liner and a quantity of large pebbles. This kind of pool would probably look best in a seaside garden.

THE NATURAL CYCLE

SOIL FERTILITY

A stable natural ecosystem maintains itself in what is described as a 'dynamic equilibrium'; this means that there are changes, depending on climate and weather and the internal growth and decay within the system, but that it keeps itself pretty much in balance. A garden that borrows a natural style does not have this inherent balance, although it is several steps towards it, which means that there should be rather less maintenance that you would expect in a conventional garden. The gardener's task is to restore equilibrium if some plants seem to be getting too much out of hand, and to maintain a positive interactive cycle between people and plants, such as those that created meadowlands and woodlands. These habitats are not truly natural but modifications of the wild that have gained their own stability. The principle is to learn from natural systems and to reinterpret them for the garden. It is important to keep in mind that you are dealing with a garden rather than a piece of wilderness and that you yourself are part of the living system.

In a wilderness, the soil is kept fertile through the long-term decay of organic matter from plant and animal debris. Maintenance in the garden also produces detritus in the form of prunings, surplus plants and weeds. The best thing to do is to mix this material with organic waste from the kitchen to make compost, which is a fast-track version of natural recycling. The compost goes back onto the garden where it is needed. Characteristic poor soil plants, such as thyme, lavender and rosemary, do not require extra fertilizing or conditioner (although parsley, mint and chives appreciate more fertile conditions), but most garden soils benefit from the addition of rich organic matter.

A regime of making and using home-produced compost is simple, once a routine has been established. Leaf mould which improves soil structure is even more straightforward. I also use natural liquid seaweed and seaweed meal, which are natural products harvested from the common seaweed, *Ascophyllum nodosum*, on a sustainable basis. The next best thing to home-made compost is composted bark, which can be used as a supplement. Natural waste products from commercial processes (such as mushroom compost straw and cocoa shells) can also be used, but may contain pesticide residue, necessitating thorough composting before use.

BELOW **Lemon balm (*Melissa officinalis*), purple sage (*Salvia officinalis* 'Purpurescens'), thyme (*Thymus vulgaris*) and parsley (*Petroselinum crispum*) in a crisp group with contrasts of colour and texture.**

OPPOSITE **A rich mixture of loose-knit naturalistic planting in wonderful health in an organic garden. The rose 'New Dawn' makes a backdrop with the rose 'Constance Spry', with golden hop growing in front of it and tall, royal-blue anchusa, yellow *Anthemis tinctoria* 'Iden', *Erysimum* 'Bowles Mauve' starting to seed and bronze fennel just beginning to become bushy.**

NATURAL SOIL CONDITIONERS

Compost supplies all the regular needs of the garden with nitrogen (N), phosphate (P_2O_5) and potash (K_2O); (N for roots, P for shoots, and K for flowers and fruits), as well as a full range of trace elements. Essentially, in applying compost, you are returning to the soil what you have taken out in terms of fruits and other produce, flowers, prunings and weeding. It stimulates plant growth and improves the soil structure, stabilizing and buffering it against pH changes and the effects of the weather. I take a bucket of compost with me every time I put in a new plant or do some weeding or sowing, supplying the soil little and often. I find this keeps the fertility level as high as I need it, but other gardeners like to do a once- or twice-a-year spread of compost over the whole garden. Conventional gardeners complain they do not have enough compost but, in fact, they probably overuse it. Two or three bins (each roughly 1 cu m (1 cu yd) capacity), kept going on a steady rotation, should be enough for most purposes.

Animal manures make a useful addition to the garden, but they need to be fully composted before application to get rid of weed seeds and residual contaminants. Bird manures are extremely rich in nitrogen and, layered into the compost heap, help to keep it hot and working. Straw manures from horses and cattle are fine as long as they are not intensively managed, although they usually contain a high level of weed seeds. A typical analysis would estimate composted manure to have a slightly higher nitrogen content and to be about the same in phosphate and lower in potassium than home-produced compost. It is best to avoid intensive- and factory-farmed waste. The soiled bedding from guinea-pig, gerbil and rabbit hutches can all go on the compost heap.

Leaf mould can be made very simply in wire-net bins or perforated plastic bags – or in large heaps if you have a sheltered place and room. It decays slowly, generally taking about two to three years, but is lovely to work with and a splendid soil conditioner when made. There are biological activators now available that will speed up the process without any apparent detriment. Adding grass mowings will also accelerate the result.

Mushroom compost from organic sources makes an excellent soil conditioner, although it is quite alkaline and therefore not suitable for plants that normally prefer acid soils. It is usually lower in potassium than home-made compost, but has a full range of other requirements, including trace elements. There is also the possibility of a mushroom crop from spores still contained in the compost.

Bark products may be worth buying for special purposes. Plain rough-chipped bark is good for paths and children's play areas, to soften falls and protect the ground beneath from compaction. It will slowly rot down, when you will need to replenish it; or, as the children grow up, return the ground to plants. Bark also makes a good mulch for shrub beds in areas where you do not get round to weeding very often. Composted bark helps build up soil structure, but does not contain nearly so many nutrients as home-produced compost. Making your own chippings by cutting and chopping prunings and garden waste

BELOW Only a cat can be simultaneously relaxed and alert. Chipped composted bark provides a soft path, very suitable for this woodland-edge scene, with the lovely bark of Tibetan cherry (*Prunus serrula*) as a high point. The bark will rot down gradually, when it can be shovelled on to the beds, and replaced.

with a shredder is a more immediate recycling route, but the chips look less ornamental than uniform commercial bark. In my opinion, it is safer and more beneficial to pass the shreddings through the compost heap. The new generation of quieter shredders, that pulverize rather than chop, are far less likely to jam, making the task more agreeable. Shredded material composts more quickly than intact twigs because the material is in smaller pieces and more exposed to the composting micro-organisms, and because the inner surfaces are exposed to them rather than the tougher outside surfaces. When using quantities of shredded twigs and wood, it is helpful to add soft materials, such as grass cuttings and foliage (and possibly an activator) to keep the compost moist.

Cocoa shell is a by-product from chocolate production. It can be dug in or used as a mulch, but only around fairly mature plants since the salts it contains may damage young plants (there is also some indication that it can harm domestic pets). It is high in potash, average for phosphate and lowish in nitrogen. Peat was once used as a conditioner, but as it is both ineffective and means destroying a natural landscape that is not easily replaceable, it can no longer be recommended.

It is easy to over-apply a chemical fertilizer and to damage both the plants and the soil, but a well-rotted compost or manure has an in-built balance. A barrowload of compost should be roughly right for 3–4 sq m (32–43 sq ft) of soil, depending on how good the soil is to start with and its composition. Dry, hot, light soils will probably require a couple of

applications, as this is hungry ground. In a natural-style garden light regular attention is preferable to heavy single dressings usually recommended. Crop plants, such as vegetables, salads and fruit, require rather more than other plants. If you suspect there may be some pesticides in your base material, make sure you compost it for at least six months; if it then smells good and has a good concentration of compost worms, it should be fit to use.

It is always better to keep the ground covered by plants than to leave bare soil that is readily colonized by weed species in the growing months and open to the elements in winter. If you have taken up some late-season salad or vegetable plants, sow a green manure that will act as a living blanket all winter and can be composted or chopped up *in situ* with a sharp spade and turned into the soil to fertilize it for the next crop. Such manures are increasingly available to the domestic gardener and include alfalfa, winter or field beans, clovers, bitter lupin and winter tares. Choose the plants for the time of year that your ground will be free, so as to suit your soil requirements and the severity of the winter.

Comfrey is a large handsome perennial. It is also a superb compost activator. The leaves can be rotted down and diluted (10:1 to 20:1) as a foliar spray for tomatoes, peppers, squashes, peas and beans, as well as for perennials. Diluted seaweed (available commercially) is also excellent as a foliar spray and to water-in young plants. The root systems of bare-rooted plants also profit from a seaweed bath before planting. It contains complex compounds that stimulate the active life of the soil, and plant growth.

ABOVE LEFT **Comfrey, especially the kind known as *Symphytum x uplandicum*, provides leaves that are a useful ingredient for good compost heaps. Comfrey can also be steeped in water and made into a garden tonic. It grows quickly and the leaves can be harvested twice or three times a year.**

ABOVE RIGHT **A patch of winter tares, an excellent green manure that can make a quick crop over winter, as well as in spring or summer. The stemmy plants can either be chopped with a sharp spade and dug in or pulled and transported to a compost heap. Green manures provide nutrient and structure to soil or compost.**

HOW TO MAKE A COMPOST BIN

The famous E-shape compost bin is easy to make and provides excellent compost. It can be constructed from waste wood (old wooden pallets are a good source of wood) or more durably with a brick E and wooden front slats. Two or three bins 1m (3ft) in height, depth and width should ensure a steady supply. Compost can take between three months and a year to make.

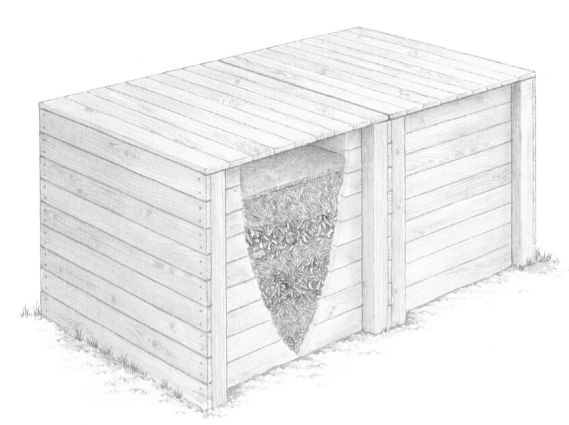

1 Fill one bin with garden and kitchen waste, keeping the surface covered flat with a piece of sacking or carpet. Try to alternate stemmy, dry material and green and wetter layers. Put in stems, prunings, shreddings, weed leaves and vegetable and fruit peelings. Avoid meat, fish, perennial weeds, roots and seeds.

2 Begin the second bin when the first is full. Turn the materials in the first bin after a month or so to aerate them – this makes the heap start working and heating up again. Turn again at intervals. Compost that has not been turned will take longer. Use when the compost is dark, crumbly and sweet-smelling.

RIGHT A triple bin for compost: the nearest one is overflowing with new sappy material, the middle one, having been turned, is well into the process of 'cooking', the one furthest away is ready to be shovelled out and put on the garden.

WATER USE AND CONSERVATION

Indulging in the regular application of quantities of water in a garden is an admission of failure. It means unquestionably that you have got your choice of plants wrong and that your soil is incapable of sustaining the plants throughout periods of stress. There may be occasional points of urgency, for example, in times of prolonged drought and heat, when certain plants will demand special attention. In this event, watering thoroughly to the base of a plant is the best means of delivering water; however, if you find yourself having to do this often, think of revising your design to create a more humid microclimate or simply to substitute plants that are suited to dry conditions. Repeated shallow watering and automatic spraying brings roots to the surface and creates a dependency on artificial watering. Drip-watering systems are currently being heavily promoted by the manufacturers, but these too create a water dependency and, being on a large scale, use a considerable amount of water.

The current wisdom on climate warming means that gardeners will need to be alert to the comfort of their plants. Above all, keeping the soil in good, organically rich condition means that plants will be able to find more moisture and will be cushioned against climatic stress.

Certain plants, such as some vegetable crops, young seedlings and newly planted items, will have a special need for water. Preferably this should be supplied by rainwater, and recent innovations in plastic technology make it simple to attach a valved fitment on to a rainwater downpipe. With this system, water running from the roof is diverted into a water barrel until the barrel is full, at which point it takes its normal course to the drain. Underwater tanks are also used as larger reservoirs which are capacious, cool and hidden out of sight. A small pump, such as the ones used in garden ponds, can be used to bring up the water when it is needed.

SEEDS AND SEEDLINGS

The natural garden, with its emphasis on plants that self-seed and naturalize, needs a special touch when it comes to new plants. Those that are bought from nurseries and garden centres need to fit happily into one of your preferred habitats, as well as into the overall design of the garden. When they are first planted they will need watering until they are established. Even stout perennials and shrubs can be at risk when they are young and first transplanted, so

it is wise to keep the area around the base thoroughly weeded until you judge the plant is robust enough to stand up to competition. Container grown plants should have their peat-based standard compost gently washed away before being planted with the correct mixture of loamy garden soil and compost.

Seedlings should be cherished, which means that garden hoes can be discarded in favour of tools that allow the gardener to be more discriminating. Self-sown seedlings sometimes grow in the most fortuitous places, creating effects and associations you could not have dreamed of. They also get themselves into totally awkward situations – growing through the back-door mat or blocking a fall of steps, or simply out of place in the overall design of the garden. These will have to be removed from their original place and transplanted to a good site. Complete this procedure as quickly as possible and water the transplant in with dilute seaweed.

Self-seeding leaves the matter of propagation up to the plants. The alternative is to collect seed and to sow it yourself. Take a tip from the plants and collect

ABOVE **The first frosts hit the foliage; a later frost will knock most of it back to the ground. Evergreens will stay upright and the opaque silver moons of honesty may survive into the spring – as long as a flock of hungry finches does not spot it.**

COLLECTING AND DRYING SEED

Seed may be derived from a number of sources. Gathering the seed from your own garden is the most convenient because you can wait for the moment when it is precisely ripe. If friends offer seed from their gardens, you may find that it is slightly under-ripe.

Put the seedheads or fruits into an envelope or paper bag and start the storage procedure as soon as you get home. When gathering seed from the wild, make sure it is ripe and collect judiciously, leaving plenty of seeds where you found them.

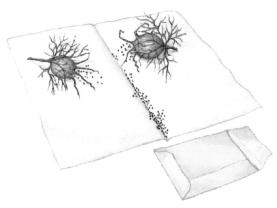

1 Gather the ripe pods, capsules or fruits – love-in-a-mist (*Nigella damascena*) is shown here – in the afternoon, when the early dews have quite dried away. Spread them on a piece of paper towel, laid on a seed tray, to dry further if necessary.

2 Make sure you distinguish seeds from bits of seedcase or pod. Gently empty all the seeds on to a sheet of white paper. Remove any that look under-ripe or damaged; tip the rest into a small paper envelope, on which you should write the name and date.

the seed when it is ripe: that is when the seedpod or capsule splits and begins to let the seeds out or they begin to drop off a seedhead. Collections should be done on a dry day and parts of the fruit, pod or capsule and other detritus cleaned away. If they are not to be sown immediately, put the seeds in an envelope and label it clearly. Store the envelopes in a tin box in a cool dry place until you need them.

Cuttings are a useful and direct means of propagation, as well as a nice gift for a friend. They are always worth a try. I have several willows, ivies, a fragrant winter honeysuckle and three hardy fuchsias that came from bouquets given me by gardening friends. Cuttings are also a good way to propagate a hedge from a single plant. Box (*Buxus sempervirens*) cuttings are slow-growing but take readily, and can be provided from clippings when you trim an original plant or hedge. You do need to remember where cuttings are placed, however, so that they are not overwhelmed by other vegetation.

Trees, shrubs, climbing plants, perennials and house plants can all be propagated by this, usually easy, method. You can grow many kinds of cutting

RIGHT **Mullein (*Verbascum phoeniceum*), growing with hostas, a form of heartsease, the wild pansy (*Viola tricolor*), and the blue spires of bugle (*Ajuga reptans*), in a quiet corner of the garden. This combination of perennials and self-seeders will more or less take care of itself.**

outdoors – precious ones can be set in pots in a cold greenhouse or a cold frame and planted outdoors later once the roots are established.

RECYCLING WITHIN THE GARDEN

The aim of a garden in a natural style is to be as self-sustaining as possible. A woodland-edge area of the garden will have its own leaf fall, although it can also be enriched by applications of leaf mould. This can be turned into the soil during weeding and placed around plants such as hellebores and hardy geraniums in early spring, when new growth is just beginning to show.

Compost is welcome almost anywhere, but especially in prairie borders, mixed beds and places where you grow vegetables and fruit. If there is any to spare, a raked and spiked lawn will enjoy the tonic of compost lightly sprinkled over it in autumn. (Dried seaweed can also be used as a top dressing in spring or autumn.) Hot, dry beds will benefit from any additional compost worked into the soil. It is easy to forget that hedges also like an application of compost or manure to their base every few years, the frequency depending on the health and vigour of the hedge. It is beneficial to apply manure or compost after a hedge has been hard-pruned.

Comparative trials recently carried out in Britain with a range of identical plants showed that most plants grew and flowered extremely well without the application of artificial fertilizers – indeed some actually did better. Lavender, which is known to prefer a dry, well-drained, poor soil, did marvellously in the unfed plot, as would be expected, but roses, argyranthemums, grasses and Chilean glory vine (*Eccremocarpus scaber*) exceeded all expectations and flowered prolifically. As well as lavenders, shrubs such as broom, buddleja, ceanothus and rosemary actually seem to thrive more in a poor soil. Annuals such as Californian poppies (*Eschscholzia californica*), cosmos and echiums also seem to do well and flower rather earlier in poorer soil conditions.

Meadow plants do not like improved soil, so it is important to remember to mow the meadow area after the plants have flowered and to rake off the mowings. It seems to be best if the meadow flowers are allowed to seed in some, but not all, years.

Prairie meadows, which do not have a grass matrix and where the plants are more densely planted, benefit from compost or leaf mould applied in spring. It is also worth remembering, that although weeds can get established in a rich, organic

soil, it is much easier to hook them out. Even really difficult weeds with deep interconnecting strings of roots, such as couch grass and bindweeds, come out quite readily in a good soil.

If you really enjoy your garden and walk around it frequently – even if only while you drink a cup of tea or snatch a quick breakfast or evening drink – you will see how your plants are keeping and be quickly alert to any influx of pests or special needs in terms of water or extra compost. You can also revel in the tiny changes that take place from day to day. A garden that is cultivated and managed in a natural style should give you time and opportunity to enjoy the natural pleasures of gardening.

ABOVE **Too wild for some tastes – a tumble of annual and perennial plants, and clumps of purple loosestrife (*Lythrum salicaria*), grasses and shrubs, interspersed with field scabious (*Knautia arvensis*) and self-seeded annuals, such as the field poppy (*Papaver rhoeas*) and borage (*Borago officinalis*).**

PLANT AND HABITAT GUIDE KEY

These tables summarize some of the practical characteristics of
a selection of plants suitable for the habitats mentioned in this
book. Take this as a starting point and use a guide, such as a
plant encyclopaedia, to fill out the detail, remembering that no
plant or garden is entirely typical or standard and that there
will always be surprises.

ESp Early Spring	Au Autumn	✳ **half hardy** plant can withstand
Sp Spring	EAu Early Autumn	temperatures down to 0°C (32°F)
LSp Late Spring	LAu Late Autumn	✳✳ **frost hardy** plant can withstand
ESu Early Summer	EWi Early Winter	temperatures down to -5°C (23°F)
Su Summer	Wi Winter	✳✳✳ **fully hardy** plant can withstand
LSu Late Summer	LWi Late Winter	temperatures down to -15° (5°F)

botanical name	height and spread	description	season	zone	hardiness	origin
HOT, DRY PLACES						
SHRUBS						
Artemisia 'Powis Castle'	H60cm/2ft s40–80cm/16–32in	evergreen; clumps of feathery silvery foliage	Su	8	✳✳	Mediterranean
Cistus x *cyprius*	H2m/6ft s1.5m/5ft	large white flowers blotched gold and crimson at base	Su	7	✳✳✳	Mediterranean
Euphorbia characias subsp. *characias*	H/s1.2m/4ft	evergreen; dense bluish foliage; rich lime-green heads	Sp	7	✳✳✳	Mediterranean
Lavandula angustifolia 'Hidcote'	H60cm/24in s75cm/30in	compact, grey-green foliage; deep purple flowers	Su	7	✳✳✳	Mediterranean
Perovskia atriplicifolia 'Blue Spire'	H/s1.2m/4ft	Russian sage; misty spires of violet-blue flowers; grey-green foliage	LSu	6	✳✳✳	C Asia
Phlomis fruticosa	H/s1m/3ft	evergreen; mounding aromatic grey-green leaves; yellow flowers	Su	7	✳✳✳	Mediterranean
PERENNIALS & BULBS						
Alstroemeria ligtu hybrids	H60cm/24in s75cm/30in	bright flowers like tiny lilies; tuberous roots; slow to establish	Su	6	✳✳✳	Chile, Argentina
Canna indica	H1.5–2.2m/5–7ft s50cm/20in	bright-flowered rhizomatous plant	Su	8	✳	Asia, Americas
Coreopsis verticillata 'Moonbeam'	H50cm/20in s30cm/12in	feathery dark leaves; yellow daisy-like flowers – long season	Su	5	✳✳✳	Maryland–N Carolina
Eryngium x *tripartitum*	H60cm/24in s50cm/20in	spiny blue-green thistle; small violet flowerheads on branched stems	Su	5	✳✳✳	Mediterranean
Gaura lindheimeri	H80cm/32in s90cm/35in	graceful with ink-tinged white butterfly-like flowers	LSu	7	✳✳✳	Texas, Louisiana
Lilium regale	H50cm–2m/20in–6ft	tall erect leafy stems; white, pink-flushed trumpets	Su	5	✳✳✳	W China

Canna indica

Eschscholzia californica

Rosa x *odorata* 'Mutabilis'

botanical name	height and spread	description	season	zone	hardiness	origin
PAVING CREVICES						
Corydalis ochroleuca	H30cm/1ft S30cm/2ft	evergreen; fern-like foliage; clusters of ivory tubular flowers	Sp/Su	5	✲✲✲	SE Europe
Papaver somniferum	H75cm/30in S30cm/12in	opium poppy; self-seeding poppy in various colours; annual	Su	4	✲✲✲	Unknown
Thymus pulegioides	H5–25cm/2–10in S30cm/12in	aromatic small leaves; pink-purple whorled flowers	ESu	5	✲✲✲	Europe
Verbascum blattaria f. *albiflorum*	H1m/39in S20cm/8in	self-seeding, elegant biennial; dark green foliage; white/pinkish flowers	Su	6	✲✲✲	C Asia, Europe
POTS						
Argyranthemum frutescens	H/S80cm/32in	daisy flowers; feathery foliage; many species and hybrids	Su	9	✲	Canary Islands
Eschscholzia californica	H30cm/12in S15cm/6in	bright silky-flowered poppies	Sp/Au	6	✲✲✲	California

WALLS

botanical name	height and spread	description	season	zone	hardiness	origin
SHRUBS AND CLIMBERS						
Buddleja davidii	H3m/10ft	buddleja; sweet-scented dense panicles of lilac flowers	Su	7	✲✲✲	China, Japan
Choisya ternata	H/S2.5m/8ft; prune to size	Mexican orange blossom; glossy green foliage; clusters of scented white flowers	Sp/Au	7	✲✲✲	SW USA, Mexico
Clematis montana	H7m/23ft S3m/10ft	good for shaded walls, poor soils; scented; will grow into trees	ESu	7	✲✲	China
Cytisus battandieri	H4m/12ft	pineapple broom; bright yellow flowers; silvery green foliage	Sp	8	✲✲✲	Garden origin
Rosa 'Félicité Perpétue'	H4.5m/15ft S3m/10ft	creamy white, double, scented flowers; good in poor soil and shade	Su	7	✲✲✲	France
Rosa 'Seagull'	H7.5m/25ft S4.5m/15ft	multiflora rambler; gold-centred flowers with double white petals	Su	7	✲✲✲	Britain
WALL BASE						
Allium roseum	H10–65cm/4–26in S5cm/2in	good for rock walls, will grow on summit and around base	Su	7	✲✲✲	Europe, N Africa
Corydalis ochroleuca	H/W30cm/12in	evergreen; ivory tubular flowers; ferny foliage	SpSu	5	✲✲✲	Europe
Nerine flexuosa 'Alba'	H45cm/18in S8cm/3in	palest pink flowers with wavy margins	LAu	6	✲✲✲	South Africa
Rosa x *odorata* 'Mutabilis'	H90cm/3ft S60cm/2ft	changing honey, pink, orange single flowers; good in poor soil	All	7	✲✲✲	China
Sternbergia lutea	H16cm/6in S8cm/3in	goblet-shaped yellow flowers; dark green strappy leaves; full sun	Au	6	✲✲✲	Eurasia
Tulipa cultivars	H60cm/2ft S8cm/3in	certain named forms flower annually for years, eg. 'Apeldoorn'	MSp	7	✲✲✲	Eurasia
CREVICES						
Aubrieta 'Joy'	H10cm/4in S30cm/12in	evergreen; reliable pink-mauve cultivar with hummocks of flowers/foliage	Sp	7	✲✲✲	Eurasia
Campanula portenschlagiana	H15cm/6in S60cm/2ft	dalmation bellflower; small lavender bells; bright heart-shaped leaves	Su	7	✲✲✲	E Europe
Erigeron karvinskianus	H15-30cm/6-12in S1m/3ft	dainty daisy flowers open white, fading to pink; may self-seed	Su	7	✲✲✲	Mexico–Panama
Erinus alpinus	H8cm/3in S10cm (4in)	fairy foxglove; pink flowers; semi-evergreen; self-seeds in congenial conditions	Sp/Su	6	✲✲✲	Europe, N Africa
Erysimum cheiri	H25–45cm/10–18in S30cm/12in	wallflowers; evergreen; scented flowers	Sp	4	✲✲✲	Europe

botanical name	height and spread	description	season	zone	hardiness	origin
FERNS						
Asplenium ceterach	H15cm/6in S20cm/8in	rustyback fern; evergreen; crimped fronds with brown undersides	All	7	✱✱✱	Europe
Asplenium scolopendrium	H45–70cm/18–28in S60cm/2ft	hart's-tongue fern; evergreen; bright green, strappy leaves	All	5	✱✱✱	Eurasia, N America
Asplenium trichomanes	H15cm/6in S20cm/8in	maidenhair spleenwort; evergreen (or semi-evergreen); dark-green, pinnate fronds with wiry black stalks	All	2	✱✱✱	Subcosmopolitan

MEADOWS

botanical name	height and spread	description	season	zone	hardiness	origin
LAWN MEADOW						
Bellis perennis	H/S5–20cm/2–8in	daisy; small daisy-flowers; widely naturalized	Sp	4	✱✱✱	Europe, N America
Cardamine pratensis 'Flore Pleno'	H20cm/8in S15cm/6in	double pink flowers; kidney-shaped leaflets	Sp	4	✱✱✱	W Europe–Russia
Eranthis hyemalis	H5–8cm/2–3in S5cm/2in	winter aconite	Wi	5	✱✱✱	SE Europe
Fritillaria meleagris	H15–30cm/6–12in S8cm/3in	snake's-head fritillary; red (or white), bell-shaped pendent flowers	Sp	4	✱✱✱	Europe
Lotus corniculatus	H5–30cm/2–12in S30cm/12in+	bird's-foot trefoil; yellow-flowered perennial; naturalized N America	Su	5	✱✱✱	Eurasia
Plantago media	H15–30cm/6–12in S20cm/8in	hoary plantain; velvety leaves in rosette; pale pink flowerhead	ESp-Wi	4	✱✱✱	Eurasia
Primula veris	H/S25cm/10in	cowslip; yellow, nodding flowers	LSp	5	✱✱✱	Europe–W Asia
Primula vulgaris	H20cm/8in S30cm/12in	primrose; yellow-rosetted flower	Sp	6	✱✱✱	Eurasia
Prunella vulgaris	H10–30cm/4–12in S20cm/8in	self-heal; purple-flowered, prefers calcareous to neutral pH	Sp/Su	3	✱✱✱	Europe
Scilla bifolia	H5–20cm/2–8in S3cm/1in	squill; small bulbous perennial; deep blue flowers	Sp,	6	✱✱✱	SC & E Europe
Veronica chamaedrys	H8–15cm/3–6in S15–50cm/6–20in	germander speedwell; sky-blue twinkling flowers; naturalized N America	Sp/Su	3	✱✱✱	Europe
Vicia cracca	S1.5m/5ft	tufted vetch; scrambling or climbing blue-flowered perennial	Su	5	✱✱✱	Eurasia
SUMMER MEADOW						
Achillea millefolium	H15–30cm/8–12in S30cm/12in	yarrow; white-flowers in flat-heads	Su	2	✱✱✱	Widespread
Chaerophyllum hirsutum 'Roseum'	H/S60cm/24in	apple-scented leaves; pink flowers in flat heads	Su	6	✱✱✱	Spain– SW Russia
Chrysanthemum leucanthemum	H30–90cm/12–36in S60cm/24in	ox-eye daisy; quite variable	Su	3	✱✱✱	Europe–Asia
Cichorium intybus	H120cm/48in S60cm/24in	chicory; clear blue flowers	Su	3	✱✱✱	Mediterranean
Daucus carota	H1m/38in S30cm/12in	wild carrot; white flat-headed flowers	Su	5	✱✱✱	Widespread
Galega officinalis	H30–150cm/12–60in S90cm/36in	goat's rue; pea-like bluish flowers	Su	4	✱✱✱	CS & E Europe
Iris sibirica	H50–120cm/20–48in S20cm/8in	likes damper grass; blue-purple flowers	Su	7	✱✱✱	CE Europe
Lupinus polyphyllus and hybrids	H5–8cm/2–3in S5cm/2in	lupin; perennial species and hybrids suitable for naturalization	Su	3	✱✱✱	NW N America
PRAIRIE MEADOW						
Dierama pulcherrimum	H120cm/48in S60cm/24in	wandflower; pink flowers; long arched stem	Su	7	✱✱	S Africa
Echinacea purpurea	H150cm/60in S45cm/18in	purple cone flower; purple daisy flowers	Su	3	✱✱✱	Eurasia
Echinops ritro	H60cm/24in S45cm/18in	globe thistle; compact, clumpy silvery plant; spherical blue flowers	LSu	3	✱✱✱	CE Europe

botanical name	height and spread	description	season	zone	hardiness	origin
Eupatorium purpureum	H2m/7ft S1m/38in	Joe Pye weed; pink-purple flowers; not Australia	LSu/A	4	✳✳✳	E USA
Euphorbia characias/E.c. subsp. wulfenii	H/S120cm/48in	Blue-green foliage; brilliant lime heads	Sp/Su	7-8	✳✳✳	S Europe
Lavandula angustifolia	H1m/38in S120cm/48in	highly scented, mass of upright stems	Su	5	✳✳✳	Mediterranean
Ratibida pinnata	H120/48in S45cm/18in	grayhead cone flower; yellow daisy flowers with raised brown discs	Su/A	3	✳✳✳	N America, Mexico
Rudbeckia fulgida	H90cm/36in S45cm/18in	black-eyed Susan; bright orange-yellow daisies; 'Herbstsonne' recommended	Su/A	4	✳✳	SE USA
Santolina pinnata subsp. neapolitana	H75cm/30in S1m/38in	cotton lavender; greyish foliage, yellow flowers	Su	7	✳✳✳	S Italy
Stipa gigantea	H250cm/96in S120cm/48in	golden oats; giant feathery grass; long-lasting silvery spikes	Su	8	✳✳✳	Spain, Portugal
Thalictrum aquilegifolium	H100cm/38in S45cm/18in	meadow rue; fluffy pink flowers; delicate, fern-like leaves	Su	6	✳✳✳	Europe to Asia
Verbascum chaixii 'Album'	H90cm/36in S45cm/18in	woolly-stemmed plant; dense white flowers	Su	5	✳✳✳	ES Europe

WOODLAND EDGE

SHRUBS

botanical name	height and spread	description	season	zone	hardiness	origin
Gillenia trifoliata	H100cm/38in S60cm/24in	Bowman's root; red stems; white flowers	Su	4	✳✳✳	N America
Oemleria cerasiformis	H2.5m/8ft S4m/12ft	Elegant early-flowering shrub; small, almond-scented bell-shaped flowers hang gracefully below bright, upright leaves.	ESp	6	✳✳✳	NW America
Rubus 'Benenden'	H/S2m/6.5ft	deciduous shrub; peeling bark, large white flowers	Sp/Su	7	✳✳✳	Hybrid
Viburnum lantana	H/S3m/10ft	wayfaring tree; deciduous shrub; white flowers, red berries	Su	3	✳✳✳	Europe, N America, Asia

HERBACEOUS

botanical name	height and spread	description	season	zone	hardiness	origin
Aquilegia vulgaris	H90cm/36in S45cm/18in	columbine; originals blue – many-shaded cultivars	Su	4	✳✳✳	Europe
Astrantia major	H30–90cm/26in S45cm/18in	silver-pink, starry flowers	Su	6	✳✳✳	Eurasia
Cardamine pentaphyllos	H/S 30cm/12in	pink-lilac flowers; digitate leaves	Sp	6	✳✳✳	Europe
Cyclamen hederifolium	H13cm/5in S15cm/6in	tuberous, perennial; pink flowers, patterned leaves	Aa	6	✳✳✳	Europe

Asplenium trichomanes

Vicia cracca

Thalictrum aquilegifolium

botanical name	height and spread	description	season	zone	hardiness	origin
Digitalis purpurea	H2m/6.5ft s45cm/18in	foxglove; pink or white bells	LSu,	4	✳✳✳	Europe
Geranium phaeum	H80cm/32in s45cm/18in	dusky cranesbill; esp. purple-maroon flowers	Su	5	✳✳✳	Europe
Lysimachia punctata	H100cm/38in s30cm/12in	yellow loosestrife; whorls of yellow flowers	Su	6	✳✳✳	Europe
Meconopsis cambrica	H/s30cm/12in	Welsh poppy; yellow (sometimes orange) flowers	Sp/Au	6	✳✳✳	W Europe
Tiarella cordifolia	H20cm/8in s30cm/12in	foam flower; profuse white flowers; bright green leaves	Su	3	✳✳✳	N America

BULBS & TUBERS

botanical name	height and spread	description	season	zone	hardiness	origin
Erythronium revolutum	H20–30cm/8–12in s10cm/4in	trout lily; glossy-spottyleaved; pink lily-like flowers with thrown-back sepals	Sp	3	✳✳✳	N California
Erythronium dens-canis	H10–15cm/4–6in s10cm/4in	dog's-tooth violet; smaller single flowers	Sp	3	✳✳✳	Europe
Galanthus nivalis	H20cm/8in s8cm/3in	snowdrop; white drop flowers	ESp	4	✳✳✳	Europe
Hyacinthoides non-scripta	H30cm/12in s8cm/3in	bluebell, Spanish bluebell; naturalizes well	Sp	5	✳✳✳	Europe
Narcissus pseudonarcissus	H30cm/12in s15cm/6in	wild daffodil; *cyclamineus* also naturalizes well	Sp	4	✳✳✳	Europe

DRY SHADE

SHRUBS & PERENNIALS

botanical name	height and spread	description	season	zone	hardiness	origin
Cornus canadensis	H15cm/6in s spreading	dwarf cornel; whorled leaves; white flowers	Su	2	✳✳✳	NE America
Geranium macrorrhizum	H45cm/18in s60cm/24in	hump-forming hardy geranium; pink flowers; scented leaves	ESu	4	✳✳✳	S Europe
Iris foetidissima	H/s 60cm/24in	long, narrow, evergreen leaves; orange seedpods	Su	5	✳✳✳	Europe, Africa
Lunaria annua	H90cm/36in s30cm/12in	honesty, purple-flowered annual, decorative seedpods	Sp/Su	7	✳✳✳	Europe
Rubus 'Betty Ashburner'	H30cm/12in s spreading	prostrate, evergreen, dark glossy leaves; white flowers	Su	7	✳✳✳	hybrid
Symphytum ibericum	H30cm/12in s spreading	green leaves; cream, red-tipped flowers	LSp	5	✳✳✳	Caucasus
Tolmiea menziesii 'Taff's Gold'	H30cm/12in s spreading	gold-threaded soft leaves; greeny flowers	Su	7	✳✳✳	NW America
Trachystemon orientalis	H60cm/24in s45cm/18in	large leaved; blue-purple flowers	Su	6	✳✳✳	E Europe
Vinca minor	H20cm/8in s spreading	evergreen; sprawling foliage; blue or white flowers	Sp/Su	4	✳✳✳	Europe, Russia

Astrantia major

Erythronium revolutum

Crocosmia masoniorum

WATER & WETLAND

botanical name	height and spread	description	season	zone	hardiness	origin
AQUATIC						
Azolla filiculoides	H1cm/0.5in S spreading mat	fairy moss; lacy green, red in autumn	All	7	✳✳✳	N & S America
Iris laevigata 'Variegata'	H75cm/30in S30in/12in	ivory variegation; blue flowers	Su	5	✳✳✳	E Asia
Iris pseudacorus	H90cm/3ft S45cm/18in	yellow flag; yellow with brownish markings	Sp/S	5	✳✳✳	Europe
Lemna species	H1cm/0.5in S spreading mat	duckweed; tiny green floating plants forming a green mat	All	4–5	✳✳✳	Cosmopolitan
Menyanthes trifoliata	H30cm/12in S spreading	bogbean; fluffy pink flowers; trifoliate leaves	Su	3	✳✳✳	Europe, Asia, N America
Nymphaea alba	H20–30cm/6–12in S spreading	water lilies; different cultivars for deep or shallow water	Su	5	✳✳✳	Eurasia, N Africa
Nymphoides peltata	H15cm/6in S spreading	fringed water lily; yellow flowers; not to be planted in Australia	Su	6	✳✳✳	Europe, Asia, nat. USA
MARGINS & DAMP GROUND						
Astilbe hybrids	H45–90cm/18-36in S70cm/28in	astilbe; tall frothy flowers in pinks and creams	Su,	5	✳✳✳	E Asia, N America
Caltha palustris	H30cm/12in S45cm/18in	marsh marigold; gold cups; glossy leaves; self-seeds	Sp	3–7	✳✳✳	Europe, N America
Crocosmia masoniorum	H1m/38in grown in clumps	crocosmia; fanned leaves; arched red flowerspikes	Su	6	✳✳✳	S Africa
Decodon verticillatus	H1m/38in S spreading	swamp loosestrife; shrubby perennial; arching leafy stems; pink-purple flowers in dense clusters	Su	3	✳✳✳	N America
Filipendula rubra	H2.5m/8ft S1.2m/4ft	queen of the prairie; tall perennial; red stems	Su	2	✳✳✳	E America
Filipendula ulmaria	H150cm/5ft S60cm/24in	meadowsweet; creamy frothy flowers on stem tops	Su	2	✳✳✳	Europe, W Asia
Lysimachia nummularia	H5cm/2in S spreading	creeping Jenny; trailing; yellow-flowered	Su	4	✳✳✳	Europe, nat. E America
Lychnis flos-cuculi	H/S 75cm/30in	ragged robin; deep pink flowers	Su	6	✳✳✳	Europe, Siberia
Lysichiton americanus	H1m/38in S1.2m/48in	skunk cabbage; vigorous, sail-like yellow spathes	Sp	6	✳✳✳	NW America
TREES						
Alnus glutinosa	H25m/80ft S10m/30ft	common alder; grows well in wet conditions such as pondsides; good for birds	All	5	✳✳✳	Europe–Siberia
Populus balsamifera	H to 30m/100ft S5m/15ft	balsam poplar; bright green, balsam-scented young leaves	Sp/ Su	2	✳✳✳	N America
Salix 'Erythroflexuosa'	H5m/15ft S3m/10ft	twisted willow; twisted shoots; bright green, curly leaves	All	5	✳✳✳	Asia, China
Taxodium distichum	H20–40m/70–130ft S6–9m/20–28ft	swamp cypress; deciduous conifer, dainty foliage	All	6	✳✳✳	SE America
SHRUBS FOR DAMP GROUND						
Hydrangea arborescens	H/S2.5m/8ft	creamy flowers in large groups; broad oval leaves	LSu	3	✳✳✳	E America
Physocarpus opulifolius	H/S1.2m/4ft spreading	'Dart's Gold' ninebark; deciduous, small white flowers; prefers acid soil	ESu	2	✳✳✳	N America
Sambucus nigra f. *laciniata*	H/S2.5m/8ft	cut-leaved elder; dark green, finely-cut leaves; white flowers in flat heads	ESu	5	✳✳✳	Europe, SW Asia

INDEX

Page numbers in *italic* refer
to illustration captions.

ACKNOWLEDGEMENTS

The Publisher would like to thank the following for their kind permission to reproduce the photographs in this book:

Key : **t** top, **c** centre, **b** bottom, **l** left, **r** right

Endpapers Garden Picture Library/Ron Evans; 1 S & O Mathews; 2 Andrew Lawson Photography/Anne Dexter; 3 Andrew Lawson Photography; 4-5 Garden Picture Library/J S Sira; 6–7 S & O Mathews; 8 Garden Picture Library/Ron Sutherland; 9 Garden Picture Library/J S Sira; 10 Andrew Lawson Photography/Eastgrove Cottage; 11 Bruce Coleman Ltd/Andy Purcell; 12 Andrew Lawson Photography; 13 **t** Francesca Greenoak; **b** Clive Nichols Photography/designer: Julie Toll; 14 Garden Picture Library/Lamontagne; 15 Garden Picture Library/Kathy Charlton; 16 Garden Picture Library/Henk Dijkman; 17 **t** Andrew Lawson Photography; **b** Andrew Lawson Photography; 18 **l** S & O Mathews, **r** Andrew Lawson Photography; 19 Jerry Harpur; 20 **t** Garden Picture Library/Alan Bedding; **b** Andrew Lawson Photography/Designer Anne Dexter; 22 Garden Picture Library/Jerry Pavia; 23 Andrew Lawson Photography; 24 Clive Nichols Photography/Designer:Mark Brown; 25 **t** Francesca Greenoak; **b** Garden Picture Library/Lamontagne; 26 S & O Mathews; 27 S & O Mathews; 28 **t** Andrew Lawson Photography; **b** S & O Mathews; 29 Jerry Harpur/Dolwen; 30 **l** Bruce Coleman Ltd/Sir Jeremy Grayson; **r** Francesca Greenoak; 31 Garden Picture Library/Steven Wooster; 32 Francesca Greenoak; 33 Reed Consumer Books Limited/Stephen Robson; 34 Garden Picture Library/John Glover; 35 Garden Picture Library/Sunniva Harte; 36 Jerry Harpur/Mr and Mrs Boyle, Home Farm, Blascote; 37 Garden Picture Library/Clive Boursnell; 38 Garden Picture Library/Marijke Heuff; 39 **l** Garden Picture Library/Michael Howes; **r** Jerry Pavia; 40 Jerry Pavia; 41 Andrew Lawson Photography; 42–43 S & O Mathews; 44 Andrew Lawson Photography; 45 Andrew Lawson Photography; 46 **t** Francesca Greenoak; **b** Andrew Lawson Photography; 48 S & O Mathews; 49 S & O Mathews; 50 Andrew Lawson Photography; 51 S & O Mathews; 52 Clive Nichols Photography/Greystone Cottage, Oxon; 53 Clive Nichols Photography; 54 Garden Picture Library/Sunniva Harte; 55 Garden Picture Library/Ron Evans; 56 Clive Nichols Photography/Abbotswood, Gloucestershire; **r** Andrew Lawson Photography; 57 S & O Mathews; 58 Garden Picture Library/Ron Sutherland; 59 S & O Mathews; 61 Garden Picture Library/Steven Wooster; 63 S & O Mathews; 64 S & O Mathews; 65 **t** Garden Picture Library/Ron Sutherland; **b** Clive Nichols Photography/Painswick Rococo Garden, Glos.; 66 Andrew Lawson Photography/Denmans Gardens; 67 Jerry Harpur/designer: Molly Love, CA; 68 S & O Mathews; 70 **l** Andrew Lawson Photography; **r** Andrew Lawson Photography; 71 S & O Mathews; 72 **t** S & O Mathews; **b** S & O Mathews; 73 Garden Picture Library/Juliette Wade; 74 S & O Mathews; 75 **t** Jerry Harpur/designer: D Gaboulaud; **b** Andrew Lawson Photography; 76 Garden Picture Library/Jerry Pavia; 77 **t** Garden Picture Library/John Glover; **b** S & O Mathews; 78 Garden Picture Library/Lamontagne; 79 **l** Jerry Harpur/designer: Roger Raiche, S.F.; **r** Andrew Lawson Photography; 80 Jerry Harpur/Great Dixter; 81 Andrew Lawson Photography; 83 Garden Picture Library/Kathy Charlton; 84 Jerry Harpur/Great Dixter; 85 **t** S & O Mathews; **b** Francesca Greenoak; 86 S & O Mathews; 87 **t** Andrew Lawson Photography/The Garden House/Buclkand Monachorum, Devon; **b** S & O Mathews; 88 **t** Garden Picture Library/Ron Evans; **b** Andrew Lawson Photography; 89 Jerry Harpur/designer: Mirabel Osler; 90 Applewood Seed Company.; 91 Applewood Seed Company.; 92 Garden Picture Library/Gary Rogers; 93 **t** Bruce Coleman Ltd/John Shaw; **b** Garden Picture Library/J S Sira; 94–5 Clive Nichols Photography/designer: H M P Leyhill; 96 Andrew Lawson Photography; 97 Garden Picture Library/JS Sira; 98 Garden Picture Library/John Glover; 99 Jerry Harpur; 100 **l** S & O Mathews; **r** Andrew Lawson Photography/designer: Arne Maynard; 101 S & O Mathews; 102 Garden Picture Library/Sunniva Harte; 103 **t** Garden Picture Library/John Miller; **b** Reed Consumer Books Limited/Stephen Robson/Occidental Arts and Ecology Centre, California; 104 Garden Picture Library/Henk Dijkman; 105 **t** Garden Picture Library/Artist: Peter Gough Ph:Sunniva Harte; **b** William Pye; 106 Jerry Harpur; 107 Andrew Lawson Photography; 108 **t** Andrew Lawson Photography; **b** Stiffkey Lamp Shop; 110 S & O Mathews; 111 Garden Picture Library/Mayer/Le Scanff; 112 Garden Picture Library/Juliet Greene; 113 Garden Picture Library/Mayer/Le Scanff; 114 **t** Francesca Greenoak; **b** Garden Picture Library/Brigitte Thomas; 115 Garden Picture Library/JS Sira; 116 N.H.P.A./Stephen Dalton; 117 Andrew Lawson Photography; 118 S & O Mathews; 119 **t** Reed Consumer Books Limited/Stephen Robson; **b** N.H.P.A./Robert Erwin; 121 Andrew Lawson Photography; 122 Jerry Harpur/desgner: Mirabel Osler; 123 Andrew Lawson Photography; 124 **l** N.H.P.A./Laurie Campbell; **r** Bruce Coleman Ltd/G. Ziesler; 125 **t** Bruce Coleman Ltd/Mike Price; **b** Aquila Photographics/Wayne Lankinen; 126 Aquila Photographics/Abraham Cardwell; 127 S & O Mathews; 128 S & O Mathews; 129 Aquila Photographics/A.H. Vanhinsbergh; 130 Garden Picture Library/Brigitte Thomas; 131 Andrew Lawson Photography; 132 **l** Jerry Harpur/Designer: Susan Horseman; **r** S & O Mathews; 134 Garden Picture Library/John Glover; 135 Andrew Lawson Photography; 136 Garden Picture Library/Michael Howes; 137 **t** Garden Picture Library/Juliette Wade, **b** Andrew Lawson Photography/The Mythic Garden; 138 S & O Mathews; 139 Garden Picture Library/J S Sira; 140 Andrew Lawson Photography; 141 Jerry Harpur; 142 Garden Picture Library/Jerry Pavia; 143 **l** Garden Picture Library/J S Sira; **r** Garden Picture Library/Brian Carter; 144 **b** S & O Mathews; 145 Andrew Lawson Photography; 146 Garden Picture Library/Marijke Heuff; 147 Garden Picture Library/Geoff Dann; 148–9 Jerry Harpur 150 **l** Garden Picture Library/Sunniva Harte; **c** Garden Picture Library/Vaughan Fleming; **r** Andrew Lawson Photography; 153 **l** Garden Picture Library/Howard Rice; **c** Francesca Greenoak; **r** Garden Picture Library/Ron Evans; 154 **l** Andrew Lawson Photography; **c** Garden Picture Library/JS Sira; **r** Andrew Lawson Photography.